23 QUESTIONS ABOUT HELL

BILL WIESE

Charisma
HOUSE
A STRANG COMPANY

Most STRANG COMMUNICATIONS BOOK GROUP products are available at special quantity discounts for bulk purchase for sales promotions, premiums, fund-raising, and educational needs. For details, write Strang Communications Book Group, 600 Rinehart Road, Lake Mary, Florida 32746, or telephone (407) 333-0600.

23 QUESTIONS ABOUT HELL by Bill Wiese
Published by Charisma House
A Strang Company
600 Rinehart Road
Lake Mary, Florida 32746
www.strangbookgroup.com

Unless otherwise noted, all Scripture quotations are from the New King James Version of the Bible. Copyright © 1979, 1980, 1982 by Thomas Nelson, Inc., publishers. Used by permission.

Scripture quotations marked KJV are from the King James Version of the Bible.

Scripture quotations marked NLT are from the Holy Bible, New Living Translation, copyright © 1996, 2004. Used by permission of Tyndale House Publishers, Inc., Wheaton, IL 60189. All rights reserved.

Cover design by Justin Evans
Design Director: Bill Johnson

Library of Congress Cataloging-in-Publication Data
Wiese, Bill.
 23 questions about hell / Bill Wiese. -- 1st ed.
    p. cm.
 Includes bibliographical references (p.   ).
 ISBN 978-1-61638-027-4
1. Hell--Christianity--Miscellanea. 2. Hell--Biblical
teaching--Miscellanea. I. Title. II. Title: Twenty-three questions
about hell.

First Edition

10 11 12 13 14 — 987654321
Printed in the United States of America

Contents

Introduction..1

23 *Questions*

Introduction

AS MY WIFE AND I travel and speak at churches, schools, and conferences, we are asked many questions in regard to hell and related topics. Many of these are difficult questions facing each one of us, but in this book we will attempt to answer twenty-three of the most often-asked questions with simple and succinct answers.

Each answer is based on the Word of God, as our opinions are not important. If you will read all the contents, the combined answers will give you a much better understanding about some of life's "whys" as they relate to hell and eternity.

Even though God has given us many answers and instructions clearly in His Word, many people still struggle with these questions.

The problem is that most people do not read His Word, and thereby remain uninformed. We hope you will be inspired to search the Bible for yourselves.

By no means are we saying that we can have all the answers. God is far too big for us to fully comprehend, but He has revealed Himself and His ways in His Word. We simply will share the little we have learned, and we trust that some of our material will be information that perhaps you have never yet investigated for yourself.

There are many misconceptions and presuppositions in regard to God's character and about who goes to heaven and who doesn't. I hope these answers will give you a better understanding as to why hell exists and will clearly demonstrate that we are held accountable for our decisions in life.

God loves us, and He has given us the choice to have a relationship with Him and be blessed, or to ignore Him and suffer the consequences. It is our choice. What will you choose?

—Bill Wiese

23*Questions*

Question 1 *Isn't God mean for making hell?*

> *But God demonstrates His own love toward us, in that*
> *while we were still sinners, Christ died for us.*
>
> —Romans 5:8

WOULD YOU SAY THAT the leaders of our country are mean for constructing prisons? No, it's your choice; you don't have to go there. (See Deuteronomy 30:19; Psalms 9:17; 86:5; 145:8–9; Proverbs 11:19, 21; John 3:16; Romans 5:8; 2 Peter 2:9; Revelation 20:13–15.)

Besides, hell was not prepared for man but for the devil and his angels (Matt. 25:41). God never intended for man to go there. Even now, He is preparing a place for us in heaven (John 14:2). It is only by man's stubborn will that he rejects the provision God has made for our access into heaven. It is arrogant of man to desire to go to heaven yet demand his own terms of access. If you want to live in God's house, you come by His way and not your own (Luke 13:3; John 3:36; 14:6; Acts 4:12; Rom. 10:9–10; 1 Tim. 2:4–6).

Why is hell so horrific? Because God's attributes are not present there. Many do not realize that the good we all enjoy is from God. *Good* doesn't exist apart from Him. James 1:17 states, "Every good gift and every perfect gift is from above, and comes down from the Father of lights."

The same word, *hetoimazo*, is used in Matthew 25:41, where God *prepared* hell for the devil, as is used in John 14:2, where Jesus says, "I go *to prepare* a place for you" (emphasis added). God prepared heaven as His eternal home, filled with all the attributes of His holiness and glory. But in God's preparation of hell, He removed all of His attributes, or goodness, from that place of torment. Spiritual death means to be separated from God, and to be separated from Him is to be separated from all good. As a consequence, this is the result:

▶ Hell is dark because God is light (1 John 1:5).

▶ Hell is only death because God is life (John 1:4).

▶ Hell is hatred because God is love (1 John 4:16).

▶ Hell has no mercy because the mercy of the Lord is in the heavens (Ps. 36:5).

▶ Hell is only weakness because the Lord is the giver of strength (Ps. 18:32).

▶ Hell is loud because "My people will dwell in...quiet resting places" (Isa. 32:18).

▶ Hell has no water because water is the rain of heaven (Deut. 11:11).

▶ Hell has no peace because Christ is the Prince of Peace (Isa. 9:6).

The good we experience is because God allows us to enjoy it while we are here on the earth. Psalm 33:5 states, "The earth is full of the goodness of the LORD."

However, if you want nothing to do with God, then there is a place prepared that has nothing to do with His goodness. His presence is there (Job 26:6; Ps. 139:8; Prov. 15:11; Rev. 14:10–11), in that it is before His face. However, His goodness and influence are removed.

He looks down upon it from heaven (1 Kings 8:30; Job 22:12; Ps. 11:4; 33:13; 102:19; 123:1; Prov. 15:3; Eccles. 5:2). Of course, God is in all places and sees all. I am simply saying that He has withdrawn His goodness from hell.

Proverbs 15:29 says, "The LORD is *far* from the wicked." In 2 Thessalonians 1:8–9 we read, "In flaming fire taking vengeance on those who do not know God, and on those who do not obey the gospel of our Lord Jesus Christ. These shall be punished with everlasting destruction from the presence of the Lord and from the glory of His power."

> Cast out from the presence of the Lord is the idea at the root of eternal death, the law of evil left to its unrestricted working, without one counteracting influence of the presence of God, who is the source of all light and holiness.[1]
>
> —*COMMENTARY CRITICAL AND EXPLANATORY ON THE WHOLE BIBLE*

> Essentially, hell is the place where all aspects of the presence of God will be completely withdrawn forever.[2]
>
> —HENRY M. MORRIS AND MARTIN E. CLARK

Dr. Robert Peterson said in his book *Hell on Trial*, "God is not present in hell in grace and blessing...He is present in hell, not in blessing, but in wrath."[3]

However, there is one additional thing in hell. God's wrath is present in the form of fire. The fires of hell are representative of His wrath (Deut. 32:22; Ps. 11:6; 21:8–9; Isa. 30:33; 33:14; 34:9; 66:24; Jer. 4:4; Mal. 4:1; Matt. 13:49–50; 18:8; Mark 9:43; John 15:6; Jude 7; Rev. 14:10–11; 20:10–15). The reason for this wrath is because sin must be punished (Rom. 6:23). God took out His anger on sin at the cross, as He poured out His wrath on Jesus (Ps. 22; Isa. 53; Matt. 17:12; Mark 9:12; Luke 9:22; 17:25; 24:26, 46; Heb. 9:26; 1 Pet. 2:24). However, if we don't acknowledge Him and receive Him as our Lord, then we will take the punishment (2 Thess. 1:9–10; 2 Pet. 2:9; Rev. 14:10–11; 20:13–15). It is our choice.

Most of the other terrible things in hell are not experienced because of His wrath but because of His absence—the absence of His attributes and goodness (Prov. 15:29; 2 Thess. 1:9). We need to understand that *good things* are not just here by a series of coincidental random events but because they emanate from the presence of God (Ps. 90:2; Matt. 5:45; Luke 6:35; Col. 1:16; 1 Tim. 6:17). When some say that hell is only "separation from God," as if that is no big deal, we can now grasp what that really means.

Many will look at the trees, the sky, the ocean, and so forth and comment, "Isn't Mother Nature wonderful?" Well, it is not "Mother Nature," but rather, "Father God" who provided all of the beauty we enjoy.

Just as prisons have been constructed to protect the innocent from those who are breakers of the law here on Earth, hell has been prepared for the offenders of God's law. The simple solution is, don't break God's law. "Unless you repent you will all likewise perish" (Luke 13:3; see also John 3:36; Rom. 10:9–10). Proverbs 27:12 says:

> A prudent man foresees evil and hides himself; the simple pass on and are punished.

Remember this point: Just as prisons were not the first thing in mind when men came to this country, so too hell wasn't God's first intent when He made the earth and man. Nevertheless, hell exists— and it will be your own fault if you go there.

Salvation is a free gift, but we must receive it in order to be saved. God loves you and is a good Father. He is trying to keep you out of hell and to divert you from your misguided course.

> The Spirit of the Lord GOD is upon Me,
> Because the LORD has anointed Me
> To preach good tidings to the poor;
> He has sent Me to heal the brokenhearted,
> To proclaim liberty to the captives,
> And the opening of the prison to those who are bound.
>
> —ISAIAH 61:1

23 *Questions*

Question 2 *You Christians are narrow-minded; isn't there more than one way to heaven?*

He who believes in the Son has everlasting life; and he who does not believe the Son shall not see life, but the wrath of God abides on him.

—JOHN 3:36

NO, THERE IS ONLY one way (John 3:36; 14:6; Acts 4:12; 1 Tim. 2:5).

Let me give you an analogy: Say you invited me over to your home for dinner. You gave me clear directions to your home. "Go south on Highway 95; turn right at Main Street; go to the top of the hill, and you will arrive at my house." You explain, "That is the only way to my home."

I then tell you, "I'm going to go north on 95 and turn right at Beach Boulevard because I think all roads lead to your house."

You explain, "Bill, you are not going to get to my house that way."

In the same way, God gives us clear directions to His house. I think God knows where He lives! All we have to do is follow His clear directions, and we will arrive there. That is not being narrow-minded, but rather, specific (Isa. 45:22; Hos. 13:4; John 3:36; 14:6; Acts 4:12; Eph. 2:8–9; 2 Thess. 1:9; 1 Tim. 2:5; 1 John 1:7–9; 4:15).

It may seem to be politically incorrect to say there is only one way, *but it is the truth*. Why can we accept one way for so many other things in life, but when it comes to heaven, we suddenly develop a loose, anything-goes attitude?

An airplane can only fly one way. The wing must be configured a certain way to create updraft. It must also be a certain size and shape. The correct amount of thrust must be applied in order to cause the law of lift to supersede the law of gravity. There are many other examples in life. Yet, being definite and precise in regard to spiritual matters is looked at as myopic.

A doctor tells you that you have a disease and are going to die. The only way you can live is if you take this pill, the only known cure. Would you refuse to take the pill simply because there is only one remedy (John 14:6; Acts 4:12; 1 Tim. 2:5)? No, you would be grateful for the cure. You have the choice to take the pill and live or to refuse it and die. It's up to you, not the doctor. He can only offer it. There are only two choices—we either accept the remedy or reject it.

In his book *Where Was God?* Dr. Erwin Lutzer gives an excellent correlation:

> After the news of the *Titanic*'s tragedy reached the world, the challenge was how to inform the relatives whether their loved ones were among the dead or the living. At the White Star Line's office in Liverpool, England, a huge board was set up; on one side was a cardboard sign: "Known to Be Saved," and on the other, a cardboard sign with the words, "Known to Be Lost." Hundreds of people gathered to intently watch the updates. When a messenger brought new information, those waiting held their breath, wondering to which side he would go and whose name would be added to the list.
>
> Although the travelers on the *Titanic* were either first-, second-, or third-class passengers, after the ship went down there were only two categories: the saved and the drowned. Just so, we can divide people into many different classes based on geography, race, education, and wealth. But on the final Day of Judgment, there will be only two classes: the saved and the lost. There is only heaven and hell.[1]

You can believe your own opinion, or you can believe Jesus. He said in John 14:6, "I am the way, the truth, and the life. No one comes to the Father except through Me." And Acts 4:12 says, "Nor is there salvation in any other, for there is no other name under heaven given among men by which we must be saved." It is your choice. Are you willing to gamble your most valuable asset—your soul— on simply your feelings? It would be far more prudent to base your beliefs on an established book that has been scrutinized by thousands of scholars, historians, and the like, and yet found to be true. What proof are you standing on?

> Greater love has no one than this, than to lay down one's life for his friends.
>
> —JOHN 15:13

23 *Questions*

Question 3 *Wouldn't God be mean and unloving for not allowing a good person into heaven?*

*For by your words you will be justified, and by your
words you will be condemned.*

—MATTHEW 12:37

IT IS A COMMON misconception to believe that God is mean or unloving because of His standards for entrance into heaven. A 2006 Barna poll showed that 54 percent of Americans generally believe that if you are a *good person*, you will go to heaven, and if bad, to hell.[1]

However, eternity in heaven is not based on *being good* for two reasons: First, it is based on a relationship; and second, whose standard of *good* are we referring to? Yours and mine may differ. Well, God's standard certainly does differ, as His standard is much higher than ours.

1. It is based on a relationship.

Let's look at the first reason: Suppose you knocked on the door of the most expensive home in the country and told them, "I'm moving in with you." What do you think they would say?

"No," of course! And you wouldn't expect them to welcome you. You have no relationship with them. So for you who question God's fairness, can you expect to live your entire life having nothing to do with Him, even denying that Jesus is the Son of God, and then come knocking on God's door at your death and say, "Excuse me, I'm moving in with You"?

Why would you think that you have a right to move into His house? Why should He let you in? You never asked Him to be your Father as He offered Himself to you during your life on Earth. As a matter of fact, you denied His Son as your Lord and Savior, whom He told you was the only way into heaven. Therefore, there is no relationship that exists between you and Him (John 1:12; 8:44; 17:9; Rom. 9:7–8; Gal. 3:26). He is not your Father, only your Creator (Col. 1:16). (See also John 3:36; 11:25–26; 14:6; Acts 4:12; Rom. 3:30; 10:9–10; 1 Tim. 2:5; 1 John 5:12.)

You say, "But He knows me, and He is supposed to be a loving God!" He knows you exist, but He doesn't know you personally because you didn't want to know Him. You said with your own mouth, "I don't believe that Jesus is the only way, or I don't believe He is the Son of God." It will be your own words that will send you to hell.

In Matthew 12:37, Jesus Himself said, "For by your words you will be justified, and by your words you will be condemned."

If a stranger came to you and said that he was moving into your home, would I be justified in calling you *mean* because you would not allow him access? Would I be justified in saying that you were *unloving*? No, because whether or not that person moved in with you is not based on the question of whether you are *loving* or not; it is based on your *relationship* with that person.

So it is with us. If we do not have a relationship with Jesus, then we are not in His family and have no right to enter His home. So who here is the inconsiderate and unreasonable one? Our lack of knowledge is no excuse. It is just as if we were speeding and told the police officer, "I didn't see the sign!"

Imagine showing up at the border of another country and saying to the border patrol, "Excuse me, but I'm a good person, so I would like to be granted admittance." Now, we wouldn't expect them to let us in the country, would we? So why would we expect to gain entrance into another kingdom? We need a visa or a passport for another country, and we need a relationship with Jesus for heaven. *Good* has nothing to do with it.

2. Whose standard of *good*?

Regarding our second point—"Whose standard of *good* are we referring to?"—we need to look at God's standard, and His standard of good is *perfection* (2 Sam. 22:31; Ps. 18:30; 19:7; Hab. 1:13; Matt. 5:48; Heb. 5:9; James 2:10). Based on this standard, you would need to be perfect to gain entrance into His kingdom. If you lie or steal or lust or even have a single foolish thought just once, you are excluded (Prov. 24:9; 1 Cor. 6:9; Eph. 5:5; James 2:10; Rev. 21:8). Now that's a high standard.

So let me ask you, do you meet those requirements? Are you perfect? No, no one is (Rom. 3:10, 12, 20; Gal. 2:16; 2 Tim. 1:9). Getting into heaven is not based on being good—and it's a good thing it is not. Not one of us would make it if that were the case (John 1:12; Rom. 3:20–26; 2 Cor. 5:21; Eph. 1:7; 2:8–9; 1 John 4:15). Thank God, heaven is a free gift; we can't earn it.

The only way to heaven is the Cross. Jesus said, "I am the way, the truth, and the life. No one comes to the Father except through Me" (John 14:6). I don't care what belief you were raised with, and I'm not here to denigrate anyone's belief. However, I am here to dissuade you from believing anything other than what Jesus just said. He is the only way.

Revelation 21:8 says, "But the … unbelieving … shall have their part in the lake which burns with fire and brimstone." In Matthew 7:23, Jesus said, "And then I will declare to them, 'I never knew you; depart from Me, you who practice lawlessness.'" How terrible would it be to hear that from His lips? The fact that He gives us a choice to be in relationship with Him proves He is a loving God. It is up to us to choose life.

If you want to argue with Him, you will have that opportunity on Judgment Day (Rev. 20:13–15), as Jesus will be the Judge.

> For You, Lord, are good, and ready to forgive,
> And abundant in mercy to all those who call upon You.
>
> —PSALM 86:5

23 *Questions*

Question 4 *Wouldn't you say God is unloving for sending people to hell?*

Enter by the narrow gate; for wide is the gate and broad is the way that leads to destruction, and there are many who go in by it. Because narrow is the gate and difficult is the way which leads to life, and there are few who find it.

—MATTHEW 7:13–14

GOD IS NOT SENDING anyone to hell! All of us are already on the road to hell automatically (Matt. 7:13–14; John 3:17–18). God's reason for sending His Son to Earth was to get us off that road (John 6:40; 12:47).

A 2003 Harris poll showed that 69 percent of Americans believe in hell, but only 1 percent think they will go there.[1] However, in Matthew 7:13, Jesus said, "Wide is the gate and broad is the way that leads to destruction, and there are many who go in by it."

Most do not understand that everyone is already on the road to hell (Matt. 18:3; 19:14). This is because we are all born in sin and are already condemned. John 3:18 states, "He who does not believe is condemned already." Psalm 51:5 says, "Behold, I was brought forth in iniquity, and in sin my mother conceived me." (See also Psalm 143:2; Romans 3:10, 12, 23; 5:14, 17–18; 6:23; Ephesians 1:7; 1 Timothy 2:5–6.)

If He hadn't come to die in our place, we would all end up in hell. Since we are all sinners, we cannot live in His perfect kingdom as we are. We must be given a new heart and a new spirit. We become new creatures in Christ (2 Cor. 5:17) when we trust in His Son and His shed blood for our sins (Rom. 5:8; 1 John 1:7). He will not let sinful man into heaven, as we would corrupt or defile heaven just as we have the earth (Rev. 21:27).

Some still think He is mean for allowing so many to suffer in this place of torment. But this is the same God who suffered an excruciating death on the cross to keep us out of hell. He loves everyone, even those who have denied Him and who mock Him (1 Chron. 16:34; Ezra 7:9; Ps. 119:66–68; 122:9; 143:10; 145:9; Rom. 5:8; 1 Cor. 15:3–4; Gal. 1:4; Eph. 2:4–5).

Dr. Chuck Missler said:

> The bottom line is, God does not send people to hell. People wind up in hell because they refuse to turn to Him for the forgiveness and the love provided them through the shed blood of His Son, Jesus.[2]

Most people never read the Bible to find out what it declares in regard to the entrance qualifications for heaven. We simply believe whatever we feel. Or even worse, we believe that all roads lead to heaven. This loose, sloppy approach to the way of entrance into another kingdom is simply ignorance. The percentage of those who will die is 100 percent. Yet, many take such a whimsical attitude toward something so serious. We have been given a choice—to believe Him or deny Him.

If you play a game such as Monopoly, you must play by the rules that are established. You don't apply the rules of another game when playing Monopoly, right? Why do some think God should follow our rules, and not we His? He is the designer, not us. When you get into a particular game and understand the rules, you can play with enjoyment and understanding. It makes sense to you. But before you know the rules, you have no understanding and it doesn't make sense to you. So it is with the things of God.

Some people have a warped view of God because of a negative relationship with their earthly father. This, in turn, causes them to reject a heavenly Father. Perhaps you have experienced abuse, pain, and abandonment from your father. Because of your experience, you view God and His commandments as harsh, oppressive, burdensome, and demanding.

When you hear biblical terms such as "serve" and "obey," it makes you angry. For many, to *serve* and *obey* anyone comes across with a negative connotation akin to slavery and tyranny! God looks mean and unfair—ready to hit them over the head the moment they displease Him. Yet they don't realize that the reason God wants us to serve and obey Him is so He can protect us from harm. As a result, they may steer clear of anything to do with God, church, or Christians. Because of their damaged souls, they refuse God's love and reject Him.

Others have received a twisted view of God from religion. Religion represents the father whose approval you strive for but will never receive. You are never *good enough* to receive God's love and acceptance. Religion teaches you to keep countless rules, but you never know why. You also never know God personally, and He really doesn't sound like someone you'd want to spend time with because He is too demanding.

This is not the God of the Bible. He has been extremely misrepresented over the centuries. No, God is not mean, but has provided a way for all to live with Him in heaven for all eternity. We are mean and unloving for not acknowledging His existence. To a large degree, it is the traditions that man has been taught that frame our beliefs about heaven—not God's Word. God's Word will teach us the truth about heaven if we will only read it.

The LORD is gracious and full of compassion,
Slow to anger and great in mercy.
The LORD is good to all,
And His tender mercies are over all His works.

—PSALM 145:8–9

23 *Questions*

Question 5 *Doesn't science dictate that man came from the animal kingdom?*

*And the fear of you and the dread of you shall be on
every beast of the earth, on every bird of the air, on all
that move on the earth, and on all the fish of the sea.
They are given into your hand.*

—GENESIS 9:2

I F MAN CAME FROM the animal kingdom, then where did man get a conscience?

In addition, why do most people worship God, even if their god differs from the one God of the Bible? They do so because they have an awareness of a supreme being. The animals do not. Why? Because man is made in God's image, and animals are not.

If man doesn't worship a god, then he usually worships something else, such as money, power, material things, and even himself. You will not see an animal do that! (See also Gen. 1:1, 26; John 8:9; Acts 24:16; Rom. 1:20–21; 2:15; 9:1; 2 Cor. 1:12; 4:2; 1 Tim. 1:5, 19; 1 Pet. 2:19; 3:16, 21.)

This brings me to another related issue: Some have suggested that God has an ego problem, since He demands to be worshiped. Let me clear that question up right now. First of all, God doesn't demand; He declares. He gives you a choice, but He does inform you of the consequences if you don't choose to worship Him. It is for our benefit that He tells us to worship Him. Worship is the channel of blessing. God tells us to worship Him because that is the manner in which He can bless us.

You see, man was made to worship God, and if he doesn't, he will worship something, and anything else will be harmful to him. God doesn't need our worship. If we think that He does, who here really has the ego problem? Do we really think God needs our worship, as if we are so important?

Another reason to worship Him is because *He is God*. I don't mean to sound condescending, but get a clue. God deserves our worship. He is the One giving us our next breath. We should be grateful He gives us life and that He's concerned about us. He is the Creator of the universe—and do we really have a problem worshiping Him? Hardly!

If man came from the animal kingdom, then why wouldn't he be content? He has achieved a higher positioning than all the animal kingdom and thereby "arrived," so to speak. Yet man is always striving for better and never feels satisfied. The reason? Since man was created in the image of God (Gen. 1:26), and not from a lesser form of life, he will always be striving for better.

The separation is distinct and obvious—seen in man's ability to love, his compassion, his reason, and his dominance on the planet. God gave man dominion on the earth, and He placed within the animal kingdom an innate need to fear man (Gen. 1:26–28; 9:2). Why would they fear us if we came from their species? It is only because God said it would be so. There is such a vast difference between an ape and a man. It is difficult to believe that some are unable to see the obvious.

If there is no God, then there would be no justice for the Hitlers of this world? Since there would be no judgment in the end, there would never be any justice served. If there are no consequences for our sins, then why do people strive to do what is right? If we are only from the animal kingdom, then survival of the fittest shouldn't bother us. Where does this concern for others come from? Animals do not possess that characteristic. These are legitimate thoughts and questions one needs to ponder and consider if he is a believer in evolution.

In his book *Creation*, Dr. Grant R. Jeffrey writes:

> An English theologian, William Paley, was the first person in recent centuries who articulated the "argument from design"..."There cannot be design without a designer." Paley argued that a man who discovered a watch while walking in the forest would be forced by logic and common sense to acknowledge that the complexity, the materials, and the obvious and purposeful and intricate design of the watch capable of measuring the precise passage of time led to the logical conclusion that there must be an intelligent purposeful watchmaker... Paley wrote, "The contrivances of nature surpass the contrivances of art, in the complexity, subtlety, and curiosity of the mechanism."[1]

In other words, you wouldn't say that, through the eons of time, as the winds blew, and as the sands swept across the ground, that one day this beautiful watch began forming; and after millions of years it became this perfectly made watch, keeping perfect time. No, you would not think such a foolish thought. Well, the wrist that wears the watch is far more complex. To see all the order around us, it is so very apparent that there must be a designer. Just as the watch obviously had a designer, so do we.

If someone doesn't believe in God, he usually believes that "nature" is the reason for existence. In the book *How Now Shall We Live?* Charles Colson says:

> Naturalism is the idea that nature is all that exists... In its broadest sense, naturalism can even include certain forms of religion—those in which the spiritual is conceived as completely

inherent within nature, such a neo-pagan and New Age religions... If nature is all there is, then there is no transcendent source of moral truth, and we are left to construct morality on our own. Every principal is reduced to a personal preference. By contrast, the Christian believes in a God who has spoken, who has revealed an absolute and unchanging standard of right and wrong, based ultimately on His own holy character.[2]

Either you believe in God, or you believe that it all happened by accident. If the latter is your position, then nature dictates and there is no one to whom you have to give an account. There are an increasing number of scientists who do not believe in evolution, as more evidence of design has emerged and become apparent. Even many of those who support evolution cannot explain the delicate balance of all the laws and the precision in virtually every aspect in our universe. With all this design, there must be a designer.

There is for me powerful evidence that there is something going on behind it all... It seems as though somebody has fine-tuned nature's numbers to make the Universe... The impression of design is overwhelming.[3]
    —PAUL DAVIES, PROFESSOR OF THEORETICAL PHYSICS

If one considers the possible constants and laws that could have emerged, the odds against a Universe that produced life like ours is immense.[4]
    —STEPHEN HAWKING, ASTROPHYSICIST

A common sense interpretation of the facts... suggests that a super intellect has monkeyed with physics, as well as chemistry and biology, and there are no blind forces worth speaking about in nature.[5]

—SIR FRED HOYLE, A COMMITTED EVOLUTIONIST

I find it quite impossible that such order came out of chaos. There has to be some organizing principal. God to me is a mystery but is the explanation for the miracle of existence, why there is something instead of nothing.[6]

—ALAN SANDAGE, ASTRONOMER

If the Universe had not been made with the most exacting precision, we could never have come into existence. It is my view that these circumstances indicate the Universe was created for man to live in.[7]

—JOHN O'KEEFE,
NASA ASTRONOMER, SCIENTIST, AND PROFESSOR

In his book *The Emperor's New Mind*, Dr. Roger Penrose says this about his final conclusion regarding the precise accuracy of the nature of creation: "This now tells us how precise the Creator's aim must have been, namely to an accuracy of one part in 10 to the 123rd."[8]

The ancient Greek philosophers were impressed with the order that pervades the cosmos, and many of them ascribed that order to the work of an intelligent mind who fashioned the Universe.[9]

—WILLIAM LANE CRAIG

The National Center for Science Education, whose specific function is to monitor and oppose activities of creationists, recommends that evolutionists should always decline invitations to debate creationists, acknowledging that they will probably lose the debate."...He explains, "...because there is no real scientific evidence for evolution."[10]

—HENRY MORRIS

Praise ye the LORD...Which made heaven, and earth, the sea, and all that therein is...He telleth the number of the stars; he calleth them all by their names...Who hath measured the waters in the hollow of his hand, and meted out heaven with the span, and comprehended the dust of the earth in a measure, and weighed the mountains in scales, and the hills in a balance?...Mine hand also hath laid the foundation of the earth, and my right hand hath spanned the heavens...It is he that sitteth upon the circle of the earth...that stretcheth out the heavens as a curtain...Though the LORD be high, yet hath he respect unto the lowly...Lord, what is man, that thou takest knowledge of him!...for I am fearfully and wonderfully made...How precious also are thy thoughts unto me, O God! how great is the sum of them! If I should count them, they are more in number than the sand...Praise him for his mighty acts.

—PSALMS 138:6; 139:14, 17; 144:3; 146:1, 6; 147:4; 150:2; ISAIAH 40:12; 40:22; 48:13, KJV

23 *Questions*

Question 6 *Where was God when the disaster (earthquake, tsunami, hurricane, etc.) struck?*

If My people who are called by My name will humble
themselves, and pray and seek My face, and turn from
their wicked ways, then I will hear from heaven, and
will forgive their sin and heal their land.

—2 CHRONICLES 7:14

MANY PEOPLE ARE QUICK to point a finger when disaster strikes, but in all the good times these same people deny that God even exists, much less giving Him thanks for those good times (Ps. 18:49; 30:12; Col. 1:3, 12; 1 Thess. 5:18).

Disaster does not usually come from God, as you will see in the next chapter. There are evil forces on the earth, and we must pray in order for God to intervene and stop the evil (John 10:10).

God can, of course, send a plague or disaster if He chooses, but the disaster is usually a result of one or more of the five reasons I point out in the following chapter. If God does send destruction, then it is usually because of continual rebellion and sin and after the many warnings He sent were not heeded.

For the most part, men do not pray. Yet Jesus told us to pray that His will be done on the earth as it is in heaven (Matt. 6:10). In other words, if we don't pray, His will is not always done. There are no disasters in heaven, and that is also His will for the earth. If we would pray, God would get involved to a greater degree, as prayer gives Him the access to intervene (2 Chron. 7:14).

In his book *Through the Windows of Heaven*, Dr. Walter Martin said:

Don't call into question God's attributes of mercy and compassion. Call into question the mess that we made of the earth in which we live. When God created it, it wasn't intended to be this way. The beauty that's in the world was God's idea. The mess was ours. And now, when we look around and see a world cursed by sin, and we see judgment in that world...we blame God.[1]

Dr. Erwin Lutzer said, "Often the same people who ask where God was following a disaster thanklessly refuse to worship and honor Him for years of peace and calmness. They disregard God in good times, yet think He is obligated to provide help when bad times come."[2] (See also the next question about why evil occurs.)

We live in a fallen world, and men choose to sin and disobey God every day. There are consequences for our decisions, and there are consequences for our sins. There is also a law of sowing and reaping. Destruction is a result of sin (Prov. 13:21).

In addition, God has given man the earth and has given him dominion in it (Gen. 1:28; Ps. 115:16). He also has given the born-again man power over the devil (Luke 10:19). The mess that the earth is in is not God's fault but man's. If God weren't intervening through man's prayer, then we would have all destroyed ourselves long ago.

For He [God] is kind to the unthankful and evil.

—LUKE 6:35

23_Questions_

Question 7 _If there is a God,_
then why is there
so much evil in
the world?

Be sober, be vigilant; because your adversary the devil walks about like a roaring lion, seeking whom he may devour.

—1 PETER 5:8

I F THERE IS NO God, then why is there so much good in the world? Where does the "good" come from (Ps. 33:5; Luke 6:35; 12:32; Heb. 6:5; James 1:17; 3 John 11)?

The question of evil in the world is a complex question and deserves a more comprehensive answer. This answer will be the lengthiest in comparison to the others, as an understanding of this question will help clarify the answers for the others.

The reason I believe this question is associated with hell is because many think God is the one responsible for the disasters and thereby mean enough to send people to hell. Their thought is, "If He didn't cause the tragedy, then why didn't He stop it?" This reasoning leads them to conclude that God is unloving and arbitrarily sends whomever He wants to hell. This is completely erroneous—furthermore, the evil that occurs is, for the most part, not caused by God.

Evil exists for many reasons, and here are just five:

1. Satan is the god of this world. He brings the death and destruction, not God.

2. Men have a free will to obey God and be blessed or to disobey and be cursed. It's their choice.

3. What a man sows he will reap.

4. There is a law of sin and death, and it operates just like the law of gravity.

5. The earth itself rebels against sin.

We will elaborate on each of these reasons just ahead.

We Are to Know His Ways

One of the common misconceptions is that man cannot know why evil occurs in our world. Even many Christians will respond with Isaiah 55:8–9, which says:

> "For My thoughts are not your thoughts,
> Nor are your ways My ways," says the LORD.
> "For as the heavens are higher than the earth,
> So are My ways higher than your ways,
> And My thoughts than your thoughts."

People misinterpret these verses to conclude that we cannot know the *whys* in life. However, we need to consider to whom God was speaking in that verse. In the preceding verse, He is telling us that it is "the wicked" who "forsake his way, and the unrighteous man his thoughts" (v. 7)—not His children. The wicked cannot know His ways, but we are expected to know His ways. He tells us what His will is and why evil exists.

You say, "What about the sovereignty of God?" Of course God is sovereign, but only outside His Word. In other words, He will not do anything against what He has already written, as His Word will never change (Ps. 89:34; 119:89). His written Word declares His will, and He expects us to know what it says.

For example, remember when Jesus was about to heal the woman bowed over with a crippling disease, He said, "So ought not this woman, being a daughter of Abraham, whom Satan has bound—think of it—for eighteen years, be loosed from this bond...?" (Luke 13:16). He expected them to know that she had a right to be loosed, since He said, "Ought not...," posed as a rhetorical question.

What about when Jesus came near to the city of Jerusalem, and wept, saying, "If you had known...the time of your visitation" (Luke 19:42, 44). The people were accountable to know the Scriptures (Heb. 10:7), which told of His day to enter Jerusalem as the Savior of the world (Ps. 118:21–24; Isa. 25:8–9; Zech. 9:9).

Also, when the apostles couldn't cast the demon out of the boy in Matthew 17:17, Jesus said, "O faithless and perverse generation, how long shall I be with you?" He expected that by then they should have known what He was doing and have the faith required to believe in His mission.

When Jesus was talking with the disciples about the suffering He would soon endure, Peter rebuked Him, saying, "This shall not happen to You!" (Matt. 16:22).

Jesus responded with, "Get behind Me, Satan! You are an offense to Me, for you are not mindful of the things of God, but the things of men" (v. 23). Jesus didn't say, "Well, that's all right, Peter. I know you meant well." No, He wasn't concerned about trying to make Peter feel comfortable in his error. Peter should have known the scriptures stating that Jesus had to suffer and die (Ps. 22; 34:20; 41:9; Isa. 7:14; 50:6; 53:5; Hosea 11:1; Amos 8:9; Mic. 5:2; Zech. 9:9). Jesus let Peter know that Satan was speaking through his ignorance. That was strong, and we might think that was offensive. But it was necessary for Peter to know the truth. Jesus didn't pull any punches.

Many times that is what we do. We try to ease someone's pain, which is good, but let it not be done at the expense of misrepresenting God's Word. Therefore it is up to us to find out exactly what is written, for we are held accountable for that knowledge.

If a young child is killed, many will make the comment, "Well, the good Lord took him or her home." No, that is not what the Word of God says. In Proverbs 4:10 we read, "Hear, my son, and receive my sayings, and the years of your life will be many." Psalm 91:16 states, "With long life I will satisfy him, and show him My salvation." (See also Exodus 23:26; Deuteronomy 25:15; 1 Kings 3:14; Proverbs 3:2, 16; 7:1–2; 9:11; 10:27; 19:23; 28:16; Ephesians 6:3.) You can see by those verses that God's will is for us to live long lives.

Many will ask, "Why do bad things happen to good people?" They are not really expecting an answer. It is asked as if we just can "never know." However, this lack of knowledge of His Word has led many to presume that God is also the one responsible for the evil things that occur. In our ignorance, we falsely accuse God, blaming Him for the tragedies. God is not the one who kills. He is the giver of life, not the taker of it (John 10:10).

No one will argue that it is not God's will for all to be saved, right? Why? Because that fact is clear in the Bible. In the same way, the other matters are also spelled out in His Word—just as in the verses promising long life as we listed above.

Let's take a closer look at some verses that clearly state we are to know His ways.

> But let him who glories glory in this,
> That he understands and knows Me.

—JEREMIAH 9:24

... having made known to us the mystery of His will.

—EPHESIANS 1:9

Therefore do not be unwise, but understand what the will of the Lord is.

—EPHESIANS 5:17

For this reason we also, since the day we heard it, do not cease to pray for you, and to ask that you may be filled with the knowledge of His will in all wisdom and spiritual understanding.

—COLOSSIANS 1:9

And, getting back to the fact that God is sovereign, the other point is: If you are not in His family, you have no assurance of a long life whatsoever or any promise of blessings. Deuteronomy 28:66 says, "Your life shall hang in doubt before you; you shall fear day and night, and have no assurance of life." Only when we are in His family do we have these assurances, if we appropriate them through faith and obedience.

If we don't read and study (Prov. 15:28; Col. 4:6; 2 Tim. 2:15; 1 Pet. 3:15), we won't know what His will is. Instead, we will voice our own opinion and many times falsely accuse God. Of course we cannot know all things, but for the most part, His Word declares to us His ways and His will.

Why Does Evil Occur

1. Satan is the god of this world (2 Cor. 4:4).

The first reason why evil occurs is this: Satan is the one who causes all the destruction. Here are some verses that reveal this to us:

> So ought not this woman, being a daughter of Abraham, whom Satan has bound—think of it—for eighteen years, be loosed from this bond on the Sabbath?
>
> —LUKE 13:16

> The thief does not come except to steal, and to kill, and to destroy. I have come that they may have life, and that they may have it more abundantly.
>
> —JOHN 10:10

> How God anointed Jesus of Nazareth with the Holy Spirit and with power, who *went about doing good and healing all* who were oppressed by the devil, for God was with Him.
>
> —ACTS 10:38, EMPHASIS ADDED

> . . . deliver such a one to *Satan for the destruction of the flesh*, that his spirit may be saved in the day of the Lord Jesus.
>
> —1 CORINTHIANS 5:5, EMPHASIS ADDED

> For this purpose the Son of God was manifested, that He might destroy the works of the devil.
>
> —1 JOHN 3:8

When a father came to Jesus and brought his son who had a dumb spirit, he told Jesus that "ofttimes it hath cast him into the fire, and into the waters, to destroy him" (Mark 9:22, KJV). But Jesus "rebuked the foul spirit, saying unto him, Thou dumb and deaf spirit, I charge thee, come out of him, and enter no more into him. And the spirit cried, and rent him sore, and came out of him" (v. 25, KJV). Remember, God is a good God, and it is the devil who is evil. Jesus said in Luke 9:56, "For the Son of man is not come to destroy men's lives, but to save them" (KJV).

As you can see, Satan is the one who causes the destruction, not God. To grasp this fully, the reading of these verses is imperative: Psalm 107:17; Proverbs 13:20; 16:6; 19:23; 2 Corinthians 2:10–11; Ephesians 6:2–3; James 4:7; 1 Peter 5:8. The reason I am listing these verses is because my opinions are meaningless. It is only the Word of God that has authority and is the truth.

2. Men have been given a free will.

The second reason for evil existing in the world is because men have been given a free will and can choose to obey God and be blessed, or to disobey and be cursed.

> I call heaven and earth as witnesses today against you, that I have set before you life and death, blessing and cursing; therefore choose life, that both you and your descendants may live.
> —DEUTERONOMY 30:19

> "I have recompensed their deeds on their own heads," says the Lord GOD.
> —EZEKIEL 22:31

Man has the choice, and one reason he chooses to disobey God is that he does not want to be accountable for his sin. He refuses to see the truth and will make every excuse to belittle the Word of God. It is his stubborn will that causes him to reject the gospel. These verses show us the true heart of man without God.

> For in Your sight no one living is righteous.
>
> —PSALM 143:2

> Truly the hearts of the sons of men are full of evil; madness is in their hearts.
>
> —ECCLESIASTES 9:3

> They have chosen their own ways,
> And their soul delights in their abominations...
> When I called, no one answered,
> When I spoke they did not hear;
> But they did evil before My eyes,
> And chose that in which I do not delight.
>
> —ISAIAH 66:3–4

> The heart is deceitful above all things,
> And desperately wicked;
> Who can know it?
>
> —JEREMIAH 17:9

> The pride of your heart has deceived you.
>
> —OBADIAH 3

> For the hearts of this people have grown dull.
> Their ears are hard of hearing,
> And their eyes they have closed.
>
> —MATTHEW 13:15

Darkness has blinded his eyes.

—1 JOHN 2:11

If we obey God, we will be blessed. One of the main reasons why God explicitly states in His Word that we are to obey Him is because His desire is to bless us, and He can only bless us through obedience. This is what His Word promises us:

If they obey and serve Him,
They shall spend their days in prosperity,
And their years in pleasures.

—JOB 36:11

The curse of the LORD is on the house of the wicked,
But He blesses the home of the just.

—PROVERBS 3:33

By humility and the fear of the LORD
Are riches and honor and life.

—PROVERBS 22:4

If you are willing and obedient,
You shall eat the good of the land.

—ISAIAH 1:19

He is a rewarder of those who diligently seek Him.

—HEBREWS 11:6

> And whatever we ask we receive from Him, because we keep
> His commandments and do those things that are pleasing in
> His sight.
>
> —1 JOHN 3:22

Read the twenty-eighth chapter of Deuteronomy, as it paints a very clear picture of those who obey and those who do not. You will see all the blessings or all the curses that will come upon you. It should encourage you to obey God's Word, and also it will establish the fear of God in you if you do not.

Some think that the God of the Old Testament was mean and not at all like Jesus. That is completely untrue, as God does not change (Mal. 3:6; Heb. 13:8). He has always been a loving God, but He is also a just God and a righteous Judge (Deut. 32:4; Ps. 96:13). Because He is holy, He hates sin, and sin must be dealt with (Lev. 19:2; Ps. 5:5; 119:104; Hab. 1:13; Rom. 6:23; 1 Pet. 1:16; Rev. 15:4). Look at these next verses and you will see God's heart and how He has always been forgiving and loving:

> "Return, backsliding Israel," says the LORD...
> "For I am merciful...
> Only acknowledge your iniquity,
> That you have transgressed against the LORD your God."
>
> —JEREMIAH 3:12–13

> "Run up and down every street in Jerusalem," says the LORD.
> "Look high and low; search throughout the city!
> If you can find even one just and honest person,
> I will not destroy the city."
>
> —JEREMIAH 5:1, NLT

While you were doing these wicked things, says the LORD, I spoke to you about it repeatedly, but you would not listen. I called out to you, but you refused to answer.

—JEREMIAH 7:13, NLT

When people fall down, don't they get up again?
    When they discover they're on the wrong road, don't
        they turn back?
Then why do these people stay on their self-destructive path?
    Why do the people of Jerusalem refuse to turn back?
They cling tightly to their lies
    and will not turn around.

—JEREMIAH 8:4–5, NLT

Perhaps they will listen and turn from their evil ways. Then I will change my mind about the disaster I am ready to pour out on them because of their sins.

—JEREMIAH 26:3, NLT

Don't you see how wonderfully kind, tolerant, and patient God is with you? Does this mean nothing to you? Can't you see that his kindness is intended to turn you from your sin? But because you are stubborn and refuse to turn from your sin, you are storing up terrible punishment for yourself. For a day of anger is coming, when God's righteous judgment will be revealed.

—ROMANS 2:4–5, NLT

You can see God is patient and kind and reveals Himself to people throughout their lives. They refuse Him over and over. Yet, people accuse God of sending them to hell. He is the One attempting to keep us out. He died in our place to do just that. What more would you want Him to do?

3. There is a law of sowing and reaping.

A man will receive back whatever he gives out. The way in which he treats someone is the way he will be treated. If a man sows evil things, he will reap evil. Most know this as the Golden Rule. Yet many do not follow it or realize the degree of its comprehensiveness.

We all would like the "good things" to occur in our lives. Yet many live a self-centered life and still expect the good. It doesn't work that way. We must show goodness to others (Prov. 18:24). If we are givers, we will receive. If we are takers, we will be taken from. If we sell a car and do not disclose the defects, we will get a car with defects. It is a law, and it works whether you realize it or not.

> The recompense of a man's hands will be rendered to him.
> —PROVERBS 12:14

> He who is greedy for gain troubles his own house.
> —PROVERBS 15:27

> He who sows iniquity will reap sorrow.
> —PROVERBS 22:8

> He who sows sparingly will also reap sparingly, and he who sows bountifully will also reap bountifully.
> —2 CORINTHIANS 9:6

> Whatever a man sows, that he will also reap.
> —GALATIANS 6:7

There are many stories in the Bible that clearly display this law of sowing and reaping. Many times people do not think about how they have treated someone or how they lied about someone to gain a higher position. Or perhaps they didn't look out for the other guy, and now it's their turn to be overlooked. It all comes back to you, no matter who you are and no matter how many years pass.

However, if you are a Christian, you have the provision of the power of repentance. If we repent of our sin, God will forgive us and remember them no more (Ps. 79:8; 103:12; Isa. 43:25; Jer. 31:34; Heb. 10:17). Even the reaping of sin can be stopped in many cases.

Depending on the sin, there are some circumstances that are a consequence of our sinning with which we will have to live for the rest of our lives. For example, if someone has a child out of wedlock, that person will be responsible for that child and will live with the consequences of that sin for all their days. If we say something wrong or hurtful to a loved one, that person may forgive us, but the scar may never quite heal. If we are unfaithful to our spouse, that scar would be very difficult to erase. The violation of trust is the deepest kind of wound.

However, with God, all things are possible to him who believes. God is more than willing to heal even the most difficult of situations and to work something good out of evil. Psalm 86:5 says: "For You, Lord, are good, and ready to forgive, and abundant in mercy to all those who call upon You." Jesus said in Luke 4:18: "He has sent me to heal the brokenhearted..." (See also Psalm 145:7–8; 146:7–9.) We serve a good and loving God.

4. There is a law of sin and death.

What is this law? It is a law that is just as real and that operates just as effectively as the law of gravity.

> But I see another law in my members, warring against the law
> of my mind, and bringing me into captivity to the law of sin

which is in my members... So then, with the mind I myself serve the law of God, but with the flesh the law of sin.

—ROMANS 7:23–25

For the law of the Spirit of life in Christ Jesus has made me free from the law of sin and death.

—ROMANS 8:2

Living in sin will bring death into our lives, whether we know it or not. It is a spiritual law, and it is just as effective as the physical laws. Evil will come after you and hunt you down. Evil is attracted to sin just as a magnet is attracted to metal. If we continue in sin, it will destroy us. Even a Christian can be destroyed because of a lack of knowledge (Hos. 4:6).

Let evil hunt the violent man to overthrow him.

—PSALM 140:11

Destruction will come to the workers of iniquity.

—PROVERBS 10:29

He who despises the word will be destroyed.

—PROVERBS 13:13

Evil pursues sinners.

—PROVERBS 13:21

...and sin, when it is full-grown, brings forth death.

—JAMES 1:15

When we become born again, we receive the spirit of life (John 3:3–16). We are given a new heart and a new spirit, which is made alive unto God (Ezek. 18:31; 36:26; Rom. 2:29; 6:6–8; 1 John 4:13). We have been made free from this law of sin and death (Rom. 6:18–22; 8:2; Gal. 5:1).

> Likewise you also, reckon yourselves to be dead indeed to sin, but alive to God in Christ Jesus our Lord.
>
> —ROMANS 6:11

> Therefore, my brethren, you also have become dead to the law through the body of Christ…so that we should serve in the newness of the Spirit.
>
> —ROMANS 7:4–6

> For as in Adam all die, even so in Christ all shall be made alive.
> —1 CORINTHIANS 15:22

> Therefore, if anyone is in Christ, he is a new creation; old things have passed away; behold, all things have become new.
> —2 CORINTHIANS 5:17

With this new spirit, we no longer have a desire to sin (Ps. 119:10–11; 1 John 3:9). Our bodies still might, but we renew our minds with the Word of God (Ps. 119:33), and we now control our bodies instead of our bodies dictating to us.

We actually can come, and should come, to a place where we hate sin (Ps. 119:11, 104, 113, 128; Prov. 8:13). It becomes disgusting to us. However, the degree to which we hate sin is dependent upon the degree to which our mind is renewed (Rom. 12:2; 2 Cor. 4:16; Eph. 4:23; Col. 3:10). Some Christians remain as babes and never do achieve a deeper commitment to the Lord.

5. The earth itself rebels against sin.

The land itself rebels against sin. The earth was made to hear the praises of God, not blasphemies, curses, and hatred toward Him. Those nations who do not have the God of the Bible as their God will continue to live in a cursed land and will bring destruction on themselves. They will end up in hell if they don't repent and acknowledge Jesus as Lord (Ps. 9:17; 67:5–6; 68:6). Look at these verses:

> For the land is defiled; therefore I visit the punishment of its iniquity upon it, and the land vomits out its inhabitants.
> —LEVITICUS 18:25

> Fear before him, all the earth: the world also shall be stable, that it be not moved. [Lack of fear of the Lord brings earthquakes.]
> —1 CHRONICLES 16:30, KJV

> Let the peoples praise You, O God;
> Let all the peoples praise You.
> Then the earth shall yield her increase;
> God, our own God, shall bless us.
> [Nations who don't praise the Lord will go hungry.]
> —PSALM 67:5–6

> The rebellious dwell in a dry land.
> —PSALM 68:6

The earth is also defiled under its inhabitants,
Because they have transgressed the laws,
Changed the ordinance,
Broken the everlasting covenant.
Therefore the curse has devoured the earth,
And those who dwell in it are desolate.
Therefore the inhabitants of the earth are burned,
And few men are left.

—Isaiah 24:5–6

For the land is full of adulterers;
For because of a curse the land mourns.
The pleasant places of the wilderness are dried up.
Their course of life is evil,
And their might is not right.

—Jeremiah 23:10

For we know that the whole creation groans and labors with birth pangs together until now.

—Romans 8:22

Here are some verses that show us that the earth was made to hear the praises of God.

Let the heavens rejoice, and let the earth be glad;
And let them say among the nations, "The Lord reigns."
Let the sea roar, and all its fullness;
Let the field rejoice, and all that is in it.
Then the trees of the woods shall rejoice before the Lord,
For He is coming to judge the earth.

—1 Chronicles 16:31–33

The LORD reigns;
Let the earth rejoice;
Let the multitude of isles be glad!

—PSALM 97:1

The mountains and the hills
Shall break forth into singing before you,
And all the trees of the field shall clap their hands.

—ISAIAH 55:12

When the earth hears the curses from the people or the mocking of God, it will shake, be barren and dry, and vomit out its inhabitants (Isa. 24:5–6; 33:9). These are only five reasons, and there are many more. The bottom line is, if we obey His voice, He will protect us and provide for us, even in a time of famine (Ps. 33:18–19; 37:19; Ezek. 36:29).

There is only one God, the God of the Bible. Jesus is the only way of salvation. If you don't believe this, you will reap the consequences regardless. (See also Psalm 9:17; Isaiah 43:11; 44:8; 45:6, 22; 47:4; Hosea 13:4; Mark 14:62; Luke 22:69–70; John 3:16, 36; 8:24, 58; 9:35–37; 10:30, 36; 11:25–27; 12:47; 14:6, 9; Acts 4:12; Galatians 3:20; Ephesians 1:7; 1 Timothy 2:5; 1 John 4:3; 5:11–12.)

And walk in love, as Christ also has loved us and given Himself for us, an offering and a sacrifice to God for a sweet-smelling aroma.

—EPHESIANS 5:2

2³Questions

Question 8 *Seventy years of sin—does that deserve an eternity of punishment?*

But we are all like an unclean thing,
And all our righteousnesses are like filthy rags;
We all fade as a leaf,
And our iniquities, like the wind,
Have taken us away.

—Isaiah 64:6

Y OU HAVE THE WRONG premise. Eternity is not based on time—but on relationship.

Say we served a hundred years or so of punishment. At the end of the hundred years, we would still be sinners. It is not possible to pay off our sins with time. To pay it off, so to speak, would be like saying, "God, I paid the price. I did my time, and I am now justified to stand in Your presence." Man left to himself will always be sinful and can never be justified on his own (Job 15:16; Ps. 143:2; Isa. 64:6; Rom. 3:10, 12, 20, 23). Man cannot be allowed into heaven based on time. He has to have a new spirit and a new heart. God is the only one who can give us this new heart.

There are five reasons why God cannot release someone from hell after a specific time period, and all five reasons are because He cannot violate His Word.

1. We are saved by grace through faith and not by time (Eph. 2:8–9).

2. We are saved by faith and not by sight. Once you are in hell, it would not require faith to know that God and hell exist, because you are seeing it. It is

impossible to please God without faith (Heb. 11:6), and no faith is needed once you see it.

3. "Without shedding of blood there is no remission" (Heb. 9:22). The time spent in hell cannot pay for our sins; only the blood of Jesus can do that.

4. "It is appointed for men to die once, but after this the judgment" (Heb. 9:27). If God took someone out of hell, then that would constitute two judgments. The scripture says "the judgment"—only one judgment.

5. Man's soul is eternal (Gen. 1:26), and if he rejects Jesus as his Lord and Savior, there is no other place for the soul to go. Jesus is the only way to heaven.

God cannot save anyone in any other manner than what He has already written. He will not alter, compromise, or change His Word, because His Word itself declares that He cannot. Once it was spoken, it stands forever (Ps. 89:34; 119:89). Not even one letter will ever change (Matt. 5:18).

Can you imagine people standing behind their words like that? We change what we say every day. We tell someone we will see them tomorrow, then something else comes up more important, and we cancel. Many of us have done that and more. Yet God can never change or go back on any word ever spoken, for all eternity. That is one reason why He cannot get someone out of hell. He cannot alter His Word. The way of salvation is already written (Luke 13:3; John 14:6; Rom. 10:9–10; Eph. 2:8–9; Titus 3:5).

Another reason God cannot let someone out of hell and into heaven is because that person would defile heaven. God will not allow anything into heaven that defiles, and that would be the case with man's sin nature (Ps. 51:1–5; Rom. 3:23; Rev. 21:27). The soul of man is eternal (Gen. 1:26; 35:18; Job 33:28; Ps. 26:9; Prov. 23:14; Eccles. 12:7; Isa. 38:17), and there is no other place for the soul to go but hell. There exists only heaven and hell.

Sin must be paid for, and sinful mankind chose to depend upon their own "good works." God will judge them on just that, and they will be found guilty as sinners. Their sin exists and has not been dealt with.

In *One Minute After We Die*, Dr. Erwin W. Lutzer said: "The powerful lesson to be learned is that no human being's suffering can ever be a payment for sin."[1]

Sin is extremely offensive to God (Rom. 7:13). This is because He is holy (Hab. 1:13). In the book *Hell Under Fire*, Christopher W. Morgan states: "Sin is inherently against God, who is infinite in all His perfections. Thus, sin is an infinite evil and merits endless punishment."[2] He goes on to give an analogy that shows us that the relationship with the offended party does make a difference. "If an angry teenage boy punched his mother, he would deserve more punishment than if he punched his older brother."[3] If we lie to our neighbor about our age, it would not be as severe as if we lied in a courtroom to the judge. God is infinitely greater than any person, and therefore it is extremely offensive to sin against God, and it is deserving of eternal punishment.

> God's Word here states that men and women will not think themselves to be unfairly condemned by God's righteous standard, because they will have failed to live up to their own inferior morality. None will be able to truthfully say they are justified by

their own ethical systems, for they will acknowledge they have violated even their own minimal standards. All people will then concur with God's pronouncement of their guilt.[4]

—HENRY M. MORRIS AND MARTIN E. CLARK

What is the most heinous thing a person can do in this life?... [J. P. Moreland responds] "The worst thing a person can do...is to mock and dishonor and refuse to love the person that we owe absolutely everything to, which is our Creator, God Himself. You have to understand that God is infinitely greater in His goodness, holiness, kindness, and justice than anyone else. To think that a person could go through their whole life constantly ignoring Him, constantly mocking Him by the way they choose to live without Him, saying, 'I couldn't care less about what You put me here to do. I couldn't care less about Your values or Your Son's death for me. I'm going to ignore all of that'—*that's* the ultimate sin. And the only punishment worthy of that is the ultimate punishment, which is everlasting separation from God."[5]

—LEE STROBEL

Only a sinless, eternal God can pay for our eternal sin. Jesus did that, and we cannot. Time would never suffice, as that would be works. (See Job 33:16; Proverbs 20:9; Ecclesiastes 11:9; Jeremiah 24:7; Ezekiel 11:19; 18:31; 36:26; Romans 3:24–25; 5:9; 1 John 1:7.)

...to know the love of Christ which passes knowledge.

—EPHESIANS 3:19

23*Questions*

Question 9 *Didn't Jesus preach love and acceptance?*

Unless you repent you will all likewise perish.

—LUKE 13:3

N o, HE PREACHED REPENTANCE and obedience (Matt. 12:50; Luke 8:21; 13:3).

The very first word out of the mouth of Jesus is "Repent," in Matthew 4:17. Repentance is preached all throughout the Bible, especially in the New Testament (Matt. 3:2, 8; 9:13; Mark 1:4, 14–15; 2:17; 6:12; Luke 13:3; 16:30; 17:3–4; Acts 3:19; 8:22; 13:24; 17:30; 20:21; 26:20; Rev. 2:5, 16).

Jesus did not preach acceptance of everyone's beliefs; He said He was *the only* way of salvation (John 8:24; 12:47; 14:6). He said to take up our cross and follow Him, and if we don't, we are not worthy of Him (Matt. 10:38; 16:24). In the twenty-third chapter of Matthew, He called the Pharisees "blind guides," "whitewashed tombs," "hypo-crites," "serpents," "brood of vipers," and "full of dead men's bones and all uncleanness." He asked, "How can you escape the condem-nation of hell?" (Matt. 23:33). Jesus also said in Luke 19:27, "But bring here those enemies of mine, who did not want me to reign over them, and slay them before me."

How's that for "love and acceptance"? Don't get me wrong; He did preach love and forgiveness. But there is a difference. Forgiveness requires humility. Those hypocrites displayed none of that. Jesus does not try to be politically correct by pleasing His enemies.

Acceptance of others' beliefs is not a demonstration of love, but is actually a demonstration of *tolerance*. Tolerance has become the high moral ground instead of truth.

It is interesting that today's society preaches acceptance of all, except for Christianity. Many people do not want to hear the gospel because they do not want to hear that what they are doing is sin. Today, almost nothing is considered a sin. The "sin" word is treated as *archaic* and *politically incorrect*.

When Jesus spoke to Mary Magdalene, who had been delivered from seven devils, He said, "Go and sin no more" (John 8:11). Jesus didn't say, "It's all right; just be yourself."

When He healed the man lying at the pool of Bethesda who had been sick for thirty-eight years, Jesus said to him, "See, you have been made well. Sin no more, lest a worse thing come upon you" (John 5:14). Over and over Jesus told those who came to Him, "Your sins are forgiven" (Matt. 9:2, 5–6, Mark 2:5, 9–10; Luke 5:20, 23–24; 7:48).

He told them not to sin. Today, many people would accuse Him of prejudice, narrow-mindedness, or even say He was guilty of a hate crime. But Jesus told it like it was.

Jesus also said to beware when all men speak well of you (Luke 6:26). Yet that is what is so prevalent in today's climate of *tolerance* and *acceptance*. Men seek the approval of almost every people group in order to gain votes or to be considered *caring*. This is really *compromise*, not *consideration*.

Jesus was strong and direct in His teaching, but He always taught and displayed love. The Bible states that God is love (John 3:16; Rom. 5:8; Eph. 3:19; 1 John 4:16). God is far more loving than any of us can even imagine. A loving message isn't always sweet and nice; at times it may be a rebuke or be corrective in nature. A message about hell is a message of love because it is a message of warning.

Jesus preached repentance. It takes someone humble enough to admit he is a sinner in order to repent. Repentance means to *turn from our sin* and change our ways. We are to come to God with a godly sorrow and humbly ask for forgiveness (2 Cor. 7:9). God will forgive us of anything we have done if we truly repent (Ps. 86:5).

> But God, who is rich in mercy, because of His great love with which He loved us...
>
> —EPHESIANS 2:4

2 **3** *Questions*

Question 10 *Isn't preaching "hell" using scare tactics?*

*Him we preach, warning every man and teaching every
man in all wisdom, that we may present every man
perfect in Christ Jesus.*

F PREACHING HELL IS using scare tactics, then Jesus is guilty,
because He preached hell more than anyone in the Bible. To warn
someone of impending danger is a message of love (Col. 1:28).
What lies ahead for those who haven't repented (Luke 13:3) should
scare any rational person (Jude 23). The wisest man who ever lived,
besides Jesus, was King Solomon. He said in Proverbs 27:12: "A
prudent man foresees evil and hides himself; the simple pass on and
are punished." In Matthew 10:28 Jesus said, "Fear Him who is able
to destroy both soul and body in hell."

When Hurricane Ike hit Texas, the headline of a local newspaper
read: "Certain Death to Those Who Do Not Vacate." Would you say
the writers of that article were "mean" or using "scare tactics" for
issuing the warning? No, you would be grateful. In the same way, God
is giving us fair warning. You can heed His warning and live, or ignore
it and die (Deut. 30:19; Matt. 23:33, 37–38; John 15:6; Col. 1:28).

In 2 Corinthians 5:11 Paul said, "Knowing therefore the terror of
the Lord, we persuade men" (KJV). Most commentaries agree that
even though this verse was referring to the judgment seat of Christ
(the reward seat for the Christians), Paul was also referring to the
severity of judgment and hell in general. In other words, when you
understand how severe hell really is, you will be more persuasive
with men. You will want to warn them. Again, it is because you care
for the individual, not because you want to scare them.

Here's what the commentaries say regarding 2 Corinthians 5:11.

This verse is commonly taken to mean that since Paul was aware of God's terrible judgment on sin, and the horrors of hell, he went everywhere seeking to persuade men to accept the gospel.[1]

—Believer's Bible Commentary

They needed to know about the severity of hell in order to preach out of a sense of urgency.[2]

—New Testament Survey

The terror of the Lord, not of men, motivated Paul to preach with a proper heart, not in mere outward appearance.[3]

—New Testament Survey

The coming judgment so full of terrors to unbelievers... Ministers should use the terror of the Lord to persuade men.[4]

—Jamieson, Fausset, and Brown's Commentary on the Whole Bible

Let all consider the Judgment to come, which is called, The Terror of the Lord. Knowing what terrible vengeance the Lord would execute upon the workers of iniquity, the apostle and his brethren used every argument and persuasion to lead men to believe in the Lord Jesus, to act as His disciples.[5]

—Parallel Commentary on the New Testament

This is not a message of condemnation, but one of warning.

These verses below show us God's heart toward people. He is patient and loving, far beyond what any person would be.

...come home to me again, *for I am merciful*...Only acknowledge your guilt. Admit that you rebelled against the LORD your God.

—JEREMIAH 3:12–13, NLT, EMPHASIS ADDED

"Run up and down every street...," says the LORD. "Look high and low; search throughout the city! If you can find *even one just and honest person, I will not destroy the city.*"

—JEREMIAH 5:1, NLT, EMPHASIS ADDED

Can you see the Lord's heart in the verse above? He desperately does not want to administer punishment, but He wants to show us mercy!

When they discover they're on the wrong road, don't they turn back? Then why do these *people stay on their self-destructive path? Why do the people...refuse to turn back* [even though I warned them]?

—JEREMIAH 8:4–5, NLT, EMPHASIS ADDED

Perhaps they will *listen and turn from their evil ways*. Then I will change my mind about the disaster I am ready to pour out on them *because of their sins*.

—JEREMIAH 26:3, NLT, EMPHASIS ADDED

Again and again I sent my servants, the prophets, *to plead with them*, "Don't do these horrible things that I hate so much." But my people *would not listen* or turn back from their wicked ways.

—JEREMIAH 44:4–5, NLT, EMPHASIS ADDED

> Don't you realize how wonderfully *kind, tolerant, and patient*
> God is with you? Does this mean nothing to you? Can't you
> see that his kindness is intended to turn you from your sin?
> But because you are stubborn and refuse to turn from your
> sin, *you* are storing up terrible punishment *for yourself*. For a
> day of anger is coming, when God's righteous judgment will be
> revealed.
>
> —ROMANS 2:4–5, NLT, EMPHASIS ADDED

God is a loving God, but know this: His love doesn't override His
justice.

> God's love does not drive His justice. The implementation of
> God's justice does not undermine His love. God's love and
> justice cohere.[6]
>
> —CHRISTOPHER W. MORGAN

> It is an unreasonable and unscriptural notion of the mercy of
> God that He is merciful in such a sense that He cannot bear
> that penal justice should be excused.[7]
>
> —JONATHAN EDWARDS

God is not to be taken as only this sweet, gentle lamb, as many
may think. He is all of that, but He is also a God who will pour out His
wrath on Judgment Day because of sin (Nah. 1:2, 6; Rom. 1:18; 2:5;
13:4; Eph. 5:6; Col. 3:6; 1 Thess. 2:16; 2 Pet. 2:9; Rev. 6:17; 14:10).

Take note of these next verses, because they reveal the other side
of God.

> Who knoweth the power of thine anger?
>
> —PSALM 90:11, KJV

Because I have called, and ye refused; I have stretched out my hand, and no man regarded; but ye have set at nought all my council, and would none of my reproof: I also will laugh at your calamity; I will mock when your fear cometh; when your fear cometh as desolation, and your destruction cometh as a whirlwind; when distress and anguish cometh upon you. Then shall they call upon me, but I will not answer.

—PROVERBS 1:24–28, KJV

And the people shall be as the burnings of lime: as thorns cut up shall they be burned in the fire. Hear, ye that are far off, what I have done.

—ISAIAH 33:12–14, KJV

I will tread them in mine anger, and trample them in my fury; and their blood shall be sprinkled upon my garments, and I will stain all my raiment.

—ISAIAH 63:3, KJV

For, behold, the LORD will come with fire, and with his chariots like a whirlwind, to render his anger with fury, and his rebuke with flames of fire.

—ISAIAH 66:15, KJV

And they shall go forth, and look upon the carcases of the men that have transgressed against me: for their worm shall not die, neither shall their fire be quenched; and they shall be an abhorring unto all flesh.

—ISAIAH 66:24, KJV

> Therefore will I also deal in fury: mine eye shall not spare, neither will I have pity: and though they cry in mine ears with a loud voice, yet will I not hear them.
>
> —EZEKIEL 8:18, KJV

> For the wrath of God is revealed from heaven against all ungodliness and unrighteousness of men.
>
> —ROMANS 1:18, KJV

> In flaming fire taking vengeance on them that know not God, and that obey not the gospel of the Lord Jesus Christ: who shall be punished with everlasting destruction from the presence of the Lord, and from the glory of His power.
>
> —2 THESSALONIANS 1:8–9, KJV

> ...and to reserve the unjust unto the day of judgment to be punished.
>
> —2 PETER 2:9, KJV

> Whosoever was not found written in the book of life was cast into the lake of fire.
>
> —REVELATION 20:15, KJV

Did you get that last verse? Do you know if your name is in His book? You might want to know that now rather than find out later, when it will be too late. We are better off meeting Him now as the Lamb of God who takes away the sins of the world (John 1:29) instead of the Lion of the tribe of Judah on Judgment Day (Rev. 5:5).

Some will not respond to hearing how much God loves them; they will only hear about the wrath that is to come if they refuse to repent. Jesus showed grace to the humble and the law to the proud in order to stop their mouths (Rom. 3:19; James 4:6). Jude 23 states, "But others save with fear, pulling them out of the fire." If you are scared into believing, then great—get saved however you can.

> If we confess our sins, He is faithful and just to forgive us our sins, and to cleanse us from all unrighteousness.
>
> —1 JOHN 1:9

23 *Questions*

Question 11 *Doesn't God consider my heart? I mean well!*

> *The heart is deceitful above all things,*
> *And desperately wicked;*
> *Who can know it?*

—JEREMIAH 17:9

YES, GOD DOES CONSIDER your heart, and that's the problem. The Bible says the heart is deceitful and desperately wicked (Jer. 17:9). As a matter of fact, it says, "Truly the hearts of the sons of men are full of evil; madness is in their hearts while they live" (Eccles. 9:3). So, if you are going to use that approach, you surely won't make it.

> He who trusts in his own heart is a fool.

—PROVERBS 28:26

God's opinion of our hearts is quite different from our own. We think we are pretty good; however, the natural man without God in his heart is opposed to God's ways.

> In Your sight no one living is righteous.

—PSALM 143:2

> Who can say, "I have made my heart clean,
> I am pure from my sin"?

—PROVERBS 20:9

> There is none who does good, no, not one.

—ROMANS 3:12

The Bible also mentions that our hearts can:

- ▸ Be froward (Ps. 101:4, KJV)
- ▸ Be in error (Ps. 95:10)
- ▸ Imagine mischief (Ps. 28:3)
- ▸ Be proud (Ps. 101:5)
- ▸ Utter perverse things (Prov. 23:33)
- ▸ Be desolate (Ps. 143:4, KJV)
- ▸ Contain seven abominations (Prov. 26:25)
- ▸ Devise wicked imaginations (Prov. 6:18)
- ▸ Be filled with reproach (Job 27:6)
- ▸ Be evil (Jer. 3:17)
- ▸ Be filled by Satan (Acts 5:3)
- ▸ Be secretly enticed (Job 31:27)
- ▸ Be able to walk after our eyes (Job 31:7)

The problem is with us. In Matthew 13:15 Jesus said, "For the hearts of this people have grown dull. Their ears are hard of hearing, and their eyes they have closed." The fact is that many don't want to see and understand. They have closed their eyes to the truth, and God will not override our free will. We must be willing to seek after Him while He may be found (Acts 17:27). He will give us that new heart. Ezekiel 18:31 says: "Cast away from you all the transgressions which you have committed, and get yourselves a new heart and a new spirit. For why should you die?"

When we assert, "God knows my heart," we infer that His knowing our heart should help our case. But if God were to go by our hearts, you can see that we would all be in serious trouble. Rather, in spite of knowing our hearts, He still loves us and is always seeking to reveal Himself to us (Ps. 86:5; 145:8–9).

Dr. Erwin W. Lutzer said:

> Left to ourselves, we are filled with suspicion, greed, and fear.
> We will take advantage of others to enrich ourselves; we will
> become obsessed with self-interest, caring little for the welfare
> of our neighbors...Pascal was right when he said, "There is
> nothing that we can see on earth which does not either show
> the wretchedness of man or the mercy of God."[1]

Only God can give us that heart that seeks after Him.

> Create in me a clean heart, O God.
>
> —PSALM 51:10

> Then I will give them a heart to know Me.
>
> —JEREMIAH 24:7

> I will...take the stony heart out of their flesh.
>
> —EZEKIEL 11:19

> I will give you a new heart.
>
> —EZEKIEL 36:26

Through the reading of His Word, our minds are renewed, and
we become more like Jesus. Our foolish concepts begin to fall away.
Many Christians don't read the Bible, and their thoughts and heart
can be deceived. It is a lifelong process in learning His Word in order
to become more like Him. The more of His Word we get down into our
hearts, the more loving, compassionate, and forgiving we become.

> With my whole heart I have sought You;
> Oh, let me not wander from Your commandments!
> Your word I have hidden in my heart,
> That I might not sin against You!
>
> —PSALM 119:10–11

A godly heart is a heart that desires to serve Him and that loves Him (Ps. 119:67; Prov. 3:1–5; 6:21).

> If we confess our sins, He is faithful and just to forgive us our sins and to cleanse us from all unrighteousness.
>
> —1 JOHN 1:9

23 *Questions*

Question 12 *What about the
person in the
remotest part
of the jungle
who never heard
of Jesus?*

For God may speak in one way, or in another,
Yet man does not perceive it.
In a dream, in a vision of the night,
When deep sleep falls upon men,
While slumbering on their beds . . .
He keeps back his soul from the Pit.

—JOB 33:14–15, 18

YOU DON'T HAVE TO worry about him; the Bible says God is fair and just (Deut. 32:4; Ps. 96:10, 13; Isa. 45:21; Acts 17:31). God can give men dreams and visions to keep back his soul from the pit (Job 33:18). If that person looks up at the heavens and cries out, "God, I want to know You. Please reveal Yourself in some way to me," God will give him a dream, send someone to him, or in some way make Himself known to that individual.

God warns us throughout our lives in many ways in order to keep us out of hell. Here are just five of those ways.

1. He gives us creation.

There is evidence of design all around us, in every form of life. Since design is so prevalent, there must be a designer. Creation points to a designer, and the designer is the God of the Bible. To say there is no God and that this world was all a series of coincidences is to deny sound reasoning. God holds us accountable to seek Him (1 Chron. 28:9; Acts 17:27). Since His creation makes it obvious that He does, in fact, exist (Col. 1:16), we are without excuse (Rom. 1:20).

2. He gave us a conscience.

Our conscience tells us there is a God and that there is a right and a wrong (Rom. 2:15). It is placed in us to know there is a Creator. However, man has the ability to suppress his own conscience because of a hardness that occurs from his sin. The Bible says man's conscience becomes "seared" (1 Tim. 4:2). He refuses to be held accountable for his lifestyle to God, so he believes anything but the truth, which is an attempt to ease his guilty conscience.

3. He gives us the Bible, and within its pages are the clear directions to heaven.

In the real estate business we were taught to get things in writing. Well, God did put it in writing. The Bible—a collection of sixty-six books, written by approximately forty authors over a fifteen-hundred-year period—was written about the Savior. There is not even one discrepancy that couldn't be cleared up with good scholarship, according to many experts. The Bible told the future on many occasions, and all have come to pass, just as it said.

4. He provides us with tools for learning about Him.

He has churches on every corner, missionaries scattered throughout the world, television and radio stations, teaching and preaching DVDs and CDs, and magazines, books, and other tools to make us aware of His presence and work on Earth.

Think of how many times a Christian has shared the Lord with you. God has protected us on many occasions and kept us alive to give us more time to seek Him. Look at all the good things that have worked out for us—evidences of His blessing. So many times He intervenes to help us, and we fail to even acknowledge Him in any way.

5. God will find a way to reveal Himself.

However, the Bible says if we do not believe Jesus is the Son of God, who came in the flesh to die for us, no matter who we are, we shall die in our sins (John 8:24; 1 John 4:2–3).

> I said therefore unto you, that ye shall die in your sins: for if ye believe not that I am he, ye shall die in your sins.
>
> —JOHN 8:24, KJV

> But unto them that are contentious, and do not obey the truth, but obey unrighteousness, indignation and wrath, tribulation and anguish, upon *every soul* of man that doeth evil, of the Jew first, and also of the Gentile.
>
> —ROMANS 2:8–9, KJV, EMPHASIS ADDED

> For there is no respect of persons with God. For as many as have sinned without law shall also perish without law: and as many as have sinned in the law shall be judged by the law.
>
> —ROMANS 2:11–15, KJV

> ...death reigned from Adam to Moses.
>
> —ROMANS 5:14

> He that hath the Son hath life; and he that hath not the Son of God hath not life.
>
> —1 JOHN 5:12, KJV

For further study see: John 3:36; Acts 4:12; 2 Thess. 1:9; 1 John 2:3, 5, 17; 3:4, 10, 14–15; 4:3, 14–15.

If that man in the remote jungle doesn't cry out to God to reveal Himself and doesn't believe in the Son of God as the only Savior, then he will die in his sins, as Jesus said.

> The wicked shall be turned into hell, and all the nations that forget God.
>
> —PSALM 9:17

In Job we read:

> For God may speak in one way, or in another,
> Yet man does not perceive it.
> In a dream, in a vision of the night,
> When deep sleep falls upon men,
> While slumbering on their beds...
> He keeps back his soul from the Pit.
>
> —JOB 33:14–15, 18

God even gives men dreams and visions "in order to turn man from his deed" (v. 17) and to keep him out of hell. If a man in a remote part of the world, who never heard the gospel, would just look to the skies and cry out to God to know Him, God would reveal Himself in some fashion.

There are signposts of warning all along our road of life. Many teachers and preachers have told us that there is a warning about hell in each of the two hundred sixty chapters in the twenty-seven books in the New Testament. If you equated the warnings to actual signs on the highway and equated the twenty-seven books to twenty-seven miles, there would be a signpost every five hundred forty feet, or within every six seconds when traveling at sixty miles per hour. Seeing that many signs would get anyone's attention. If we decide to drive off the bridge and ignore all those signs, it is our own fault, not God's.

Even with all these warnings, many do not want "to retain God in their knowledge," because they do not want to give up their sin. This is the case for many who still think they are "good people." Their system of values cannot measure up to God's righteous standards. Man cannot even live up to his own standards, much less the standards of a holy God. Because God is love, He consistently reaches out to man.

God will find a way to make Himself known to all of the people in our world. The more important question is this: Now that He has made Himself known to you, *who do you say Jesus is?* (See also Mark 14:62; Luke 22:70; John 8:24, 58; 9:35–37; 10:30, 36; 11:25–27; 14:6, 9; Acts 4:12.)

> That they should seek the Lord, in the hope that they might grope for Him and find Him, though He is not far from each one of us.
>
> —ACTS 17:27

Questions

Question 13 *Isn't everyone
God's child?*

But as many as received Him, to them He gave the right to become children of God, to those who believe in His name.

—JOHN 1:12

NO, ALL PEOPLE ARE not His children. This is a common misconception. As a matter of fact, if Jesus is not your Lord and Savior, then you have a father, but it is not God—it is the devil: "You are the children of your father the devil" (John 8:44, NLT). Jesus says this is true because "there's no room in your hearts for my message" (v. 37, NLT).

In other words, either God is your Father, or the devil is your father. I know that is strong language, but most don't realize that we all have a spiritual father. There are only two choices for who this is: if we haven't made Jesus our Lord and our spiritual Father, then we have allowed the devil to be our spiritual father, whether we know it or not. If you think that is foolish, then you have a right to disagree with Jesus, but it won't change the facts. It is a misnomer to assert that we are all "the children of God."

In addition to John 8:44 above, John 1:12 says, "But to all who believed him and accepted him, he gave *the right to become* children of God" (NLT, emphasis added). When Jesus was speaking to His Father in John 17:9, He said, "I pray for them. I do not pray for the world but for those whom You have given Me, *for they are Yours*" (emphasis added). According to Galatians 3:26, it is our faith or belief in *who Jesus is* that makes us children of God: "For you all are sons of God *through faith in Christ Jesus*" (emphasis added).

Ephesians 1:5 states: "God decided in advance *to adopt us into his own family* by bringing us to himself *through Jesus Christ*" (NLT, emphasis added). (See also Matthew 5:45; Luke 6:35–36; Romans 9:7–8; Galatians 4:19; Ephesians 5:1; 1 Thessalonians 5:5.)

You say, "But He knows me, and He is supposed to be a loving God!" He knows you exist, but He doesn't know you personally. In Matthew 7:23, Jesus said, "And then I will declare to them, 'I never knew you; depart from Me, you who practice lawlessness!'" How terrible it would be to hear that from His lips! The fact that He gives us a choice to be in relationship with Him or not proves He is a loving God. It is up to us to choose.

You either obey the heavenly Father and dwell in His house, or you obey the father of lies and dwell in his house. *It is your choice.* If you say, "Well, I don't believe the Bible," then just know that Revelation 21:8 says *all unbelievers* will have their part in the lake of fire. Revelation 20:15 states: "And anyone not found written in the Book of Life was cast into the lake of fire." Now you are warned, so at Judgment Day (Rev. 20:13) you shouldn't be surprised when He says, "Depart from me, ye cursed, into the everlasting fire…" (Matt. 25:41, KJV). You will be without excuse, because your own words condemn you (Matt. 12:37). (See also Matthew 5:44–45; 7:13–14; 13:41, 49–50; Luke 3:17; 6:35; John 1:12; 5:29; 8:44; 17:9; Romans 9:8; Galatians 3:26; 4:19; Ephesians 1:5; 5:1; 2 Thessalonians 1:9–10.)

> But Jesus said, "Let the little children come to Me, and do not forbid them; for of such is the kingdom of heaven."
>
> —MATTHEW 19:14

23*Questions*

Question 14 *Can't God overlook my sins?*

For the wages of sin is death, but the gift of God is
eternal life in Christ Jesus our Lord.

—ROMANS 6:23

THERE ARE TWO VERY good reasons why God cannot overlook our sins. First of all, God's nature is unlike ours. His nature is holy and is not compatible with man's (Lev. 19:2; 20:26; Ps. 18:30; 19:7; Matt. 5:48; Rev. 15:4). We would be consumed in His presence: "Our God is a consuming fire" (Heb. 12:29). What does that mean? I believe it can be best explained in an analogy.

In his book *Charles Stanley's Handbook for Christian Living*, Charles Stanley said:

> Take fire, for example. Fire is hot by nature. Fire doesn't make itself hot; it *is* hot. That is the nature of fire. If you stuck your hand in a campfire to retrieve a hot dog that fell off your stick, you would be burned. You wouldn't get mad at the fire. You wouldn't say, "I can't believe that fire burned me. I never did anything to the fire! Why would it treat me like that?" Fire and your hand are incompatible. They don't do well together.[1]

The nature of fire is to burn. In the same way, the nature of God is to consume sin. Therefore, since man is sinful, man has a problem. It is not a matter of hoping our sins are minor and will be overlooked. *Any sin*, even minor, cannot exist in His presence.

The second reason man's sins cannot be overlooked is because God is a just judge, and sin must be punished. The Bible says that sin is punishable by death (Gen. 2:16–17; Rom. 6:23). God requires sin to be paid for since He is a just God. A good judge in our land would not be considered good if he let all the criminals go free, right? He would need to exercise justice and administer the proper punishment.

In the same way, God would not be considered just if He simply let the people go free. He also cannot show partiality and say, "Well, I'm a nice guy, so I am going to let this person off easy." That wouldn't be just, and it wouldn't be fair to the injured party. God is not *partially* just and *partially* love—He is 100 percent of each. That being the case, man's sin cannot be excused. However, since God is love (1 John 4:16), He cannot leave man in this irreconcilable state. So what will God do? How does God resolve the problem of man being unable to coexist with Him in heaven?

Long before the foundations of this earth, God had already planned that He would pay the penalty for our sin. He would die in our place. This was His first step in dealing with the punishment part of the sin problem. But there still remains the fact that only a righteous person can enter heaven. How can man ever be perfect?

The truth is, he cannot on his own. In knowing this, the Lord had purposed to allow *our trust* in Him as *right standing* with God (Rom. 4:3). If we would trust in His work on the cross, and not our own works (Rom. 3:20; Gal. 2:16; Eph. 2:8–9; Titus 3:5), we would be treated as if we were perfect. Jesus, being sinless, took our sins on Himself. He exchanged His righteousness for our sin (Rom. 3:22; 5:18; 2 Cor. 5:21). His shed blood then washes away our sins (Rom. 5:9; Eph. 1:7; Col. 1:14; Heb. 9:12; 1 Pet. 1:19; 1 John 1:7). We now can stand before God *as if* we had never sinned. What an awesome plan! He made a way where there was no way. Psalm 96:13 says: "He shall judge the world with righteousness, and the peoples with His truth."

Some people complain and say, "I don't like this *one way* that you Christians preach." They should quit complaining that there is only one way and start being grateful that there *is* a way. Why do we think God should just excuse our sin? When we continue to willfully disobey God even after He told us the consequences of our sin—that we would die (Gen. 2:17; Rom. 6:23)—then we are without excuse.

Either we let Jesus take the punishment or we take it—for all eternity. It is our choice. Trust in Him or trust in yourself. If you trust in your own good works, then God will show you everything you ever did and ever thought and what you should have done. He will reveal even the intents of your heart. All will be played back on a big screen before you and before all to see. How do you think you will look?

Will you rely on your own works, or will you trust in His?

> For by grace you have been saved through faith, and that not of yourselves; it is the gift of God, not of works, lest anyone should boast.
>
> —EPHESIANS 2:8–9

23_Questions_

Question 15 _Can't God just create another place for man to go besides hell?_

> But cowards, unbelievers, the corrupt, murderers,
> the immoral, those who practice witchcraft, idol
> worshipers, and all liars—their fate is in the fiery lake
> of burning sulfur. This is the second death.
>
> —REVELATION 21:8, NLT

HE DID; IT'S CALLED *heaven*! And He prepares a place for *you* there (John 14:2). It's your fault if you miss it. The reason people ask this question is because they want to see a place that does not contain the severity of hell. If you refer to my answer in question 1, you will see that a place *less severe* cannot exist. Hell is horrific because God's attributes and goodness have been removed. All the good we experience is only because of God. James 1:17 states that "every good gift and every perfect gift is from above, and cometh down from the Father of lights" (KJV). Psalm 33:5 says, "The earth is full of the goodness of the LORD" (KJV). There is no good thing apart from God. In eternity, it is either extremely blissful with God or extremely horrific without Him. There is no in-between.

When He completed Creation, He said, "Thus the heavens and the earth, and all the host of them, were finished" (Gen. 2:1). He is not going to create another place now, because He was finished then. His Word never changes (Ps. 119:89). Remember, hell was prepared for the devil and his angels, not for man (Matt. 25:41). Also, the main reason He would not make another place is because sin must be punished, and hell is a justifiable punishment in God's eyes.

Just as our body cannot live in outer space or in the ocean, our soul can only exist in heaven or hell. There is no other place for the soul to dwell. If we refuse the provision (Jesus) for our sins, we are rejecting the only way for our soul to be saved and enter heaven. We send ourselves to hell. God gives us that choice. God is the one who carries out the actual sending to hell, but it is our own words that condemn us (Matt. 12:37).

It is difficult to think of people suffering in hell for all eternity, but in questioning God's reasons, we then place ourselves on a higher moral plane than God Himself. The Bible says His ways are perfect (Ps. 19:7–8; 119:75, 89, 128), and we have no right to find fault with Him. We may recoil at a fiery eternal hell, but we know His ways are just.

> To think of it is dreadful, and we cannot help feeling deeply for our fellow human beings who are lost. It is right that we should. We are commanded to love our enemies as well as our neighbor, for they too are created in God's image...Yet our natural compassion can very easily slip over into a dislike of the doctrine of hell itself...When we are in heaven, we will praise God for all that He accomplished by means of hell...God's just and righteous judgment will be revealed.[1]
>
> —EDWARD DONNELLY

Because of the severity of hell, there have been many who no longer hold to the traditional (and scriptural) view of eternal punishment. In their minds they have formed a God who could never allow such suffering. What they fail to realize is that God is also holy and just. Sin must be punished, and eternal punishment is justifiable if you understand how much God hates sin.

He hates it enough to punish His Son severely for it on the cross. If sin wasn't so horrific, then God could have arranged it so that Jesus was hit over the head and killed. But He had Him endure such terrible suffering because sin is "exceedingly sinful" to God (Rom. 7:13).

He tells us plainly how to get to heaven and warns us clearly of where we will go if we reject Jesus as our Lord and Savior. "But the...unbelieving...shall have their part in the lake which burns with fire and brimstone" (Rev. 21:8). If you then say, "I don't believe that," you just condemned yourself. Why would any rational person believe the opinion of his or her mind over God's Word? Heaven is His house, and if we want to live there, we must adhere to His directions for how to arrive there (John 3:36; Acts 17:30; Rom. 10:9–10).

Remember, as we pointed out in chapter 1, there is nothing good that exists apart from God. If we sin, and all of us are guilty of that, we are separated from Him forever (Gen. 2:17). We can't have the "good" without God (Ps. 16:2–3; 27:13; 33:5; 107:15; Jer. 31:14; Zech. 9:17; James 1:17), so we need to be reconciled to Him if we ever want to experience His goodness.

He has provided for that reconciliation through His Son (Rom. 11:15; 2 Cor. 5:18–20; Col. 1:21; Heb. 2:17). If you want the good, you have to take the God of the universe with it. If you don't want Him, then there is only one place prepared for you to spend your eternity (Matt. 25:41–46). What will you choose?

> In My Father's house are many mansions; if it were not so, I would have told you. I go to prepare a place for you. And if I go and prepare a place for you, I will come again and receive you to Myself; that where I am, there you may be also.
>
> —John 14:2–3

23 *Questions*

Question 16 *Wouldn't most people in hell agree to accept the Lord if given the chance?*

*Then the fifth angel poured out his bowl on the throne
of the beast, and his kingdom was plunged into
darkness. His subjects ground their teeth in anguish,
and they cursed the God of heaven for their pains and
sores. But they did not repent of their evil deeds and
turn to God.*

—REVELATION 16:10–11, NLT

THERE WILL BE MANY who will regret their wrong decision! They will remember all the times when someone shared the gospel message with them—and they failed to respond. They will remember how often they were warned by God and all the opportunities they had to listen but refused. Their humbling in hell will come only as a result of seeing and experiencing the horrors of hell—not by faith and trust in Jesus. Most would only accept Him to avoid the pain and not because of a repentant heart.

The Word is clear that God requires faith to be saved (Eph. 2:8–9). There will be no faith needed after one sees this place of torment. It will be obvious the Bible was indeed true. God's method of salvation is spelled out in the Bible, and He will not violate His Word (Ps. 89:34; 119:89). He considers our faith and trust in Him as "righteousness." In hell, no faith is needed, so it is too late for faith.

The Bible says we are saved by faith, not by sight. We are also saved by grace, not by time spent in hell. Time spent would be works, and we are not saved by works (Gal. 2:16; Eph. 2:8–9; Titus 3:5). If we spent millions of years in hell, it wouldn't matter. When we came out, we would still be sinners, and no sinner can stand before God. Our sin can only be dealt with by God's Son shedding His blood to pay for it. It took someone sinless and eternal to pay for our eternal separation from God. Jesus did that, and He is the only one who could.

There are many who will still curse Him in hell and who would continue to refuse to repent, just as Revelation 16:10–11 prophesies.

We only have one life, and the decision for Christ must be made *before we die*. Hebrews 9:27 states: "It is appointed for men to die once, but after this the judgment." We all have made some bad decisions and have regretted them. But you don't want to make a mistake about this decision, as this decision is permanent. There is no second chance, no turning back, and no appeals court. So get this one right!

> And as it is appointed for men to die once, but after this the judgment...
>
> —HEBREWS 9:27

23*Questions*

Question 17 *Can't God just put a stop to the evil that is occurring?*

*So I sought for a man among them who would make a
wall, and stand in the gap before Me on behalf of the
land, that I should not destroy it; but I found no one.*

—EZEKIEL 22:30

N O, GOD CANNOT. SINCE the time when man introduced sin into
the world (Gen. 2:17; 3:6–13; Rom. 5:12; 1 Cor. 15:21), access
has been available to demonic forces. Satan and his demons have a
legal right to work in the earth. Jesus came that we might have life,
and more abundant life, but Satan has come to kill, steal, and destroy
(John 10:10). First John 3:8 says: "For this purpose the Son of God
was manifested, that He might destroy the works of the devil." As
the people of God, we need to pray and ask God to intervene. He
won't get involved without someone praying.

Many people die prematurely because there is no one praying for
them. God looks for someone who will stand in the gap and pray
(Ezek. 22:30). Because no one stands in the gap, God's will is not
done in many lives.

Since men sin every day, and sin brings forth death (Prov. 13:21;
Rom. 6:18–22; 8:2), evil will occur automatically. For God to stop
all the evil that is occurring, He would have to take away man's free
will. However, love always allows a choice. In their book *The Bible
Has the Answer*, Henry Morris and Martin E. Clark said, "Man was
consequently created with moral freedom. But freedom to love and
trust God necessarily also means freedom to hate and reject God.
The Creator, therefore, knew before He created man, that man would
sin and thus bring the curse of death into the world (Romans 5:12).
And surely the agony of the ensuing millenniums of suffering and

death in a groaning creation (Romans 8:22) does not bring pleasure to God."[1]

Ezekiel 33:11 says, "As I live, saith the Lord GOD, I have no pleasure in the death of the wicked" (KJV). God has given the earth to man, so if it is a mess, it is man's fault (Ps. 115:16). It is man's own doing that causes the evil, and yet man blames God. God is the one warning us to obey Him in order for us to avoid the evil. How ironic that the very one who warns us of the evil is the very one who gets blamed for that evil. The earth is full of man's ignorance, but thank God it is also full of God's mercy. We should rejoice He doesn't give us what we deserve.

Due to his sin, man breaks his own hedge of protection through disobedience, and as we read in Ecclesiastes 10:8: "Whoso breaketh an hedge, a serpent shall bite him" (KJV). If we obey, we are protected; if we do not, we are subject to attack and destruction from the enemy (Deut. 28:15). God gave us the choice to obey Him and be blessed, or to disobey and be cursed (Deut. 30:19).

> If you then, being evil, know how to give good gifts to your children, how much more will your Father who is in heaven give good things to those who ask Him!
>
> —MATTHEW 7:11

23 *Questions*

Question 18 *Is the fire in hell real or metaphorical?*

Its streams shall be turned into pitch,
And its dust into brimstone;
Its land shall become burning pitch.
It shall not be quenched night or day;
Its smoke shall ascend forever.
From generation to generation it shall lie waste;
No one shall pass through it forever and ever.
                                        —ISAIAH 34:9–10

REVELATION 9:2 STATES THAT there arose a great smoke out of the pit, and "the sun and the air were darkened because of the smoke of the pit." How could a metaphorical fire or flames of mental anguish produce real smoke? It would take a literal burning fire to produce the smoke that darkened the sky, not an allegorical or metaphorical fire.

When the rich man who had been sent to hell said he wanted a drop of water to cool his tongue, he said it was because, "I am tormented in this flame" (Luke 16:24). If it were only mental anguish or something other than real fire, then why would water suffice?

The parable of the tares is an excellent example of it being literal fire. Look what the *Holman Illustrated Bible Dictionary* says in regard to those verses:

> However, there is strong evidence to indicate that literal language is used and that the Bible does in fact teach literal fire and other sufferings. The parable of the tares in Matthew 13, which discusses eternal judgment, is helpful here. The Son of man, the world, children of the kingdom, the children of the

wicked one, the devil, the end of the world, the angels, the gath-
ering—all are literal figures in the parable. It is then natural
to conclude that the burning of the tares should also be taken
literally.[1]

If you take the Word of God literally, then it is easy to arrive at an
interpretation of literal fire. I understand that there are metaphors
and idioms, but it is obvious when they are being applied, such as
in Galatians 4:24, where it is clearly spelled out to be an allegory.
Another example is where Jesus said He was the Bread of Life (John
6:48). That is a metaphor. His Word is representative of bread, and
He is the Word. There are many such metaphors and allegories in
God's Word, but they are obvious when being used. To say that *all*
the verses I have listed herein are allegorical would require some
proof.

In the book *The Bible Has the Answer,* Dr. Henry M. Morris states:
"Whenever the Bible writers used allegories or parables or other
symbolic stories, they always either said so or else made it evident
in the context."[2]

Josh McDowell and Don Stewart say in their book *Reasons*: "To
interpret figuratively we must find a good reason in the passage to
justify doing this . . . The words of a given text should be interpreted
literally if possible."[3]

Jesus mentioned hell in forty-six verses, and eighteen of those
verses were regarding the fires of hell. The word He uses for *hell* in
eleven instances is *Gehenna*. Gehenna was just outside the walls
of Jerusalem and was the city dump that burned continually. The
unclaimed dead bodies were thrown into that fire, and the wild dogs
and maggots ate the flesh. The smell was extremely putrid and foul.[4]
This is a graphic picture that Jesus wanted the people to whom He
spoke to see in order for them to recognize He was giving them a

severe and sobering warning. Why would He compare a place of burning bodies, if the fire of hell was something quite different? Look at the burning bush of Exodus 3:2. Moses saw the bush actually burning with flames of fire, and yet it wasn't consumed. It sounds similar to a body in hell. Look at all these verses:

> For a fire is kindled in mine anger, and shall burn unto the lowest hell.
>
> —DEUTERONOMY 32:22, KJV

> Brimstone shall be scattered upon their habitation...Surely such are the dwellings of the wicked, and this is the place of him that knoweth not God.
>
> —JOB 18:15, 21, KJV

> Upon the wicked he shall rain snares, fire and brimstone, and an horrible tempest.
>
> —PSALM 11:6, KJV

> You shall make them as a fiery oven in the time of your anger; the LORD shall swallow them up in His wrath, and the fire shall devour them.
>
> —PSALM 21:9

> Let burning coals fall upon them; let them be cast into the fire, into deep pits, that they rise not up again.
>
> —PSALM 140:10

> For Tophet was established of old...Its pyre is fire with much wood; the breath of the LORD, like a stream of brimstone, kindles it.
>
> —ISAIAH 30:33

Who among us shall dwell with the devouring fire? Who among us shall dwell with everlasting burnings?

—Isaiah 33:14

Its streams shall be turned into pitch,
And its dust into brimstone;
Its land shall become burning pitch.
It shall not be quenched night or day;
Its smoke shall ascend forever.
From generation to generation it shall lie waste;
No one shall pass through it forever and ever.

—Isaiah 34:9–10

"For behold, the day is coming,
Burning like an oven...
And the day which is coming shall burn them up,"
Says the Lord of hosts.

—Malachi 4:1

So it will be at the end of the age. The angels will come forth, separate the wicked from among the just, and cast them into the furnace of fire. There will be wailing and gnashing of teeth.

—Matthew 13:49

The chaff He will burn with unquenchable fire.

—Luke 3:17

And being in torments in Hades, he lifted up his eyes and saw Abraham afar off, and Lazarus in his bosom. Then he cried and said, "Father Abraham, have mercy on me, and send Lazarus that he may dip the tip of his finger in water and cool my tongue; for I am tormented in this flame."

—Luke 16:23–24

> If anyone does not abide in Me, he is cast out as a branch and is withered; and they gather them and throw them into the fire, and they are burned.
>
> —JOHN 15:6

> He shall be tormented with fire and brimstone…And the smoke of their torment ascends forever and ever; and they have no rest day or night.
>
> —REVELATION 14:10–11

> These two were cast alive into the lake of fire burning with brimstone.
>
> —REVELATION 19:20

> The devil, who deceived them, was cast into the lake of fire and brimstone where the beast and the false prophet are. And they will be tormented day and night forever and ever.
>
> —REVELATION 20:10

There are many good scholars who state that the fire in hell is not literal. They also conclude that the worms are not literal. However, Isaiah 14:11 states: "The maggot is spread under you, and worms cover you." If it is not literal and is merely representative of thoughts eating away at your mind, then why did the writer use the word *maggot* and say they would be spread under you, with worms covering you? How would "thoughts" be spread under and over someone? If it is merely a metaphor or analogy, it is a poor one.

Since the Bible mentions heaven having gates of pearl, streets of gold, and walls of precious stones, would we say that those examples are only metaphorical language and not to be taken literally? I think not! Most would agree that the pearly gates are literal. I believe that just as heaven is literal, so are the features of hell.

I saw the flames and brimstone, and I was certain it was literal. However, I am completely convinced by the many scriptures, rather than by my own empirical evidence. It is not an important issue, one way or the other.

> ... even Jesus who delivers us from the wrath to come.
>
> —1 THESSALONIANS 1:10

23 *Questions*

Question 19 *Why are the demons themselves not in torment?*

> *The devil, who deceived them, was cast into the lake
> of fire and brimstone where the beast and the false
> prophet are. And they will be tormented day and night
> forever and ever.*
>
> —REVELATION 20:10

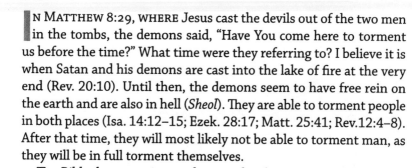

I N MATTHEW 8:29, WHERE Jesus cast the devils out of the two men in the tombs, the demons said, "Have You come here to torment us before the time?" What time were they referring to? I believe it is when Satan and his demons are cast into the lake of fire at the very end (Rev. 20:10). Until then, the demons seem to have free rein on the earth and are also in hell (*Sheol*). They are able to torment people in both places (Isa. 14:12–15; Ezek. 28:17; Matt. 25:41; Rev.12:4–8). After that time, they will most likely not be able to torment man, as they will be in full torment themselves.

The Bible, however, is not clear on this future issue. The demons seem to be in only partial torment, as many commentaries point out:

> From the words of the demons, they believed in the existence of God and the deity of Christ, as well as the reality of future judgment.[1]

> Themselves tormentors and destroyers of their victims, they discern in Jesus their own destined torments and destroyer, anticipating and dreading what they know and feel to be awaiting them.[2]

> There is a time in which devils will be more tormented than they are, and they know it. The great assize at the last day is

> the time fixed for their complete torture ... for the judgment of that day they are reserved ... They will then be made close prisoners. They have now some ease; they will then be in torment without ease. It is their own enmity to God and man that puts them upon the rack, and torments them before the time.[3]

> The fear of the demons that Christ would torment them "before the time" (v. 29) indicates that there is a future judgment for Satan and his armies.[4]

The fallen angels were thrown down to the earth (Rev. 12:4–8) and also to hell (*Sheol*).

> How you are fallen from heaven,
> O Lucifer ... cut down to the ground ...
> Yet you shall be brought down to Sheol,
> To the lowest depths of the Pit.
>
> —ISAIAH 14:12, 15

Pit, or *bowr*, is the same word used for the many verses that describe man's pit. (See *bowr*: Psalms 28:1; 30:3; 40:2; 88:4; Isaiah 38:18; Ezekiel 26:20; 31:14. *Sheol*: Psalms 49:14; 55:15; 86:13; Proverbs 15:24.) There are thirteen words for "pit" in the Old Testament, and only four (the fifth only once) are used as a synonym for *Sheol*.

Demons torment many people who are alive on the earth (Job 2:7; Matt. 8:28; Mark 5:5; 9:17–18, 22; Luke 9:39–42; 11:26; 22:31).

Demons Torment the People in Hell

Since some demons in hell are in the same place as people, and there are no angels to protect anyone (Ps. 34:7), the demons would naturally torment hell's occupants. God is the one who allows it; He is in control of hell. He assigns man his rightful position there (Matt. 24:51; Luke 12:46; Rev. 21:8).

Some have asked me, "Where in the Bible does it describe these grotesque demons you saw in hell?" The Bible describes demons and some angels, and we believe that the demons are fallen angels. I shared some information about this in my second book *Hell*.[5] Examine these next verses, and you will see a description of some of these bizarre creatures the writers described: Ezekiel 1; Revelation 4:6–8; 9:2–10; 13:11.

Here are some verses and commentary to describe the torment:

Matthew 18:34 says: "...delivered him to the tormentors" (KJV). Notice that the next verse says: "So My heavenly Father also will do to you." The question is, Who are the tormentors? Matthew Henry describes them as: "Devils, the executioners of God's wrath, will be their tormentors forever."[6]

John Wesley states: "His pardon was retracted, the whole debt required, and the offender *delivered to the tormentors forever*" (emphasis added).[7]

Luke 12:47 says: "...shall be beaten with many stripes." Regarding this verse, John Wesley states: "For the executioners of God's vengeance are at hand, and when he has once delivered you over to them, you are undone forever."[8]

Psalm 50:22 says: "Now consider this, you who forget God, lest I tear you in pieces." Matthew Henry says this about this verse: "Those that will not consider the warnings of God's Word will certainly be torn to pieces *by the executioners*."[9] Who are the executioners?

Matthew 25:41 says: "Then He will also say to those on the left hand, 'Depart from Me, you cursed, into the everlasting fire prepared for the devil and his angels.'" *Matthew Henry's Commentary on the Whole Bible* states:

If they must be doomed to such a state of endless misery, yet may they not have some good company there? No, none but the *devil and his angels*, their sworn enemies, that helped to bring them to this misery and *will triumph over them in it*. They served the devil while they lived, and therefore are justly sentenced to be where he is, as those that served closest are taken to be with him where he is. It is terrible to be in a house haunted with devils; what will it be then to be *companions with them forever*? If sinners make themselves associates with Satan by indulging in these lusts, they may thank themselves if they became sharers in that misery which was prepared for him and his associates. Then He will also say to those on the left hand, "Depart from Me, you cursed, into the everlasting fire prepared for the devil and his angels."[10]

Vine's Expository Dictionary of Old and New Testament Words states: "The abode of condemned souls and devils. The underworld place or state of *torture* and punishment for the wicked after death, *presided over by Satan*" (emphasis added).[11] Other verses regarding the torment can be found in 1 Samuel 2:10; 2 Samuel 22:6; Job 33:22; Psalms 32:10; 49:14; 74:20; 116:3; 141:7; Amos 5:18–19.

There are also many verses on the varying degrees of punishment, and many infer a tormentor (1 Sam. 2:10; Job 33:22; Ps. 50:22; Amos 5:18–19; Matt. 18:34; Luke 12:47). Matthew Henry states: "There are different degrees of punishment in that day. All the pains of hell will be intolerable, but some will be more so than others. Some sink deeper into Hell than others, and are beaten with more stripes."[12] Who is doing the beating?

Job 18:18 says: "He shall be driven from light into darkness, and chased out of the world" (KJV). Matthew Henry adds: "He is chased out of this world, hurried and dragged away by the messengers of death, sorely against his will."[13]

Job 33:22 says: "His soul draweth near to the grave [Sheol], and his life to the destroyers" (KJV). Jamieson, Fausset, and Brown call these destroyers "angels of death commissioned by God to end man's life."[14]

Revelation 14:11 says: "And the smoke of their torment ascendeth up for ever and ever: and they have no rest day nor night" (KJV). "The lost have no rest from sin and Satan, terror, torment, and remorse."[15]

Dr. Erwin Lutzer states: "It is understandable that demonic spirits would await those who enter eternity without God's forgiveness and acceptance."[16] Matthew Henry adds: "God does often, for wise and holy ends, permit the efforts of Satan's rage, and suffer him to do the mischief he would, and even by it serve his own purposes. The devils are not only Christ's captives, but his vassals."[17]

At Judgment Day (Rev. 20:10–15), Satan and his demons will be cast into the lake of fire and most likely will no longer be able to torment anyone, as they will be in full torment themselves.

Remember, Jesus delivers; Satan destroys.

> There met Him a certain man…who had demons for a long time…And they begged Him that He would permit them to enter them [the swine]. And He permitted them. Then the demons went out of the man and entered the swine, and the herd ran violently down the steep place into the lake and drowned. When those who fed him…went out to see what had happened…[they] found the man from whom the demons had departed, sitting at the feet of Jesus, clothed and in his right mind.
>
> —LUKE 8:27, 32–35

Questions

Question 20 *Since God is a loving God, all who reject Him are annihilated (and not left to suffer eternally), right?*

And these will go away into everlasting punishment,
but the righteous into eternal life.

—MATTHEW 25:46

I F GOD HAD PLANS to annihilate sinful mankind, then why did He come down and die for us? What did He save us from? No, all are not annihilated, as He made us in His image (Gen. 1:26). We will exist forever. Here are some verses that show that our soul is eternal.

...her soul was departing (for she died)...

—GENESIS 35:18

He will redeem his soul from going down to the Pit.

—JOB 33:28

Do not gather my soul with sinners.

—PSALM 26:9

For You have delivered my soul from death.

—PSALM 116:8

Do not leave my soul destitute.

—PSALM 141:8

...deliver his soul from hell.

—PROVERBS 23:14

Then the dust will return to the earth as it was, and the spirit will return to God who gave it.

—ECCLESIASTES 12:7

But You have lovingly delivered my soul from the pit of corruption.

—Isaiah 38:17

In the book *Hell Under Fire*, Christopher W. Morgan writes: "Annihilationism is the belief that those who die apart from saving faith in Jesus Christ will be ultimately destroyed. Thus, annihilationists reject the historic view of hell as conscious, endless punishment."[1]

These next verses are absolutely clear that there will be suffering in hell for all eternity.

Revelation 14:10–11 is so clear. It states: "He shall be tormented with fire and brimstone in the presence of the holy angels and in the presence of the Lamb. And the smoke of their torment ascends forever and ever; and they have *no rest day or night*" (emphasis added). Let's look at each part of these verses.

▶   "In the presence"—So this man would have to exist.

▶   "And the smoke of their torment ascends forever and ever"— Notice it says, "their torment." They must exist for the scripture to say "their torment."

▶   "…and they have no rest day nor night"—To have "no rest" you would have to exist.

In his book *Hell on Trial*, Dr. Robert A. Peterson said, "He implies their ongoing existence. It makes no sense to say that they have no rest if they have ceased to exist."[2]

Revelation 20:13 states: "Death and Hades delivered up the dead *who were in them*. And they were judged, each one according to his works" (emphasis added). You can't possibly try to get around that verse. It states the dead *who were in hell* and *were judged*. If you ceased to exist, how could you possibly be delivered up and judged? You would have to still exist, obviously. There is no getting around it.

Look at this next verse. This is proof that these two people still exist after being in the lake of fire for a thousand years. In Revelation 19:20, the beast and the false prophet are cast into the lake of fire after the Tribulation. Then at the end of the thousand years, John sees Satan being thrown into the lake of fire where the beast and the false prophet *are* (Rev. 20:10). They still exist after the thousand years—they are not annihilated.

Isaiah 14:9–10 states: "Hell from beneath is excited about you, to meet you at your coming... They all shall speak and say to you: 'Have you also become as weak as we?'" They obviously must still exist to be able to speak.

Ezekiel 32:21 states: "The strong among the mighty shall speak to him out of the midst of hell." Again, how could you speak out of hell and yet not exist?

Also, in Luke 16, the rich man said he wanted a drop of water to cool his tongue, for he was "tormented in this flame." In my book *Hell*, I cited proof that this verse is not a parable.[3] Even if it was, then how would someone draw the conclusion that no one is in hell? The parable would not make any sense and would actually imply the opposite of its intended meaning. No, it was not a parable, as two people are named, and no other parable has even one named in it. It means just what it says—that this man was alive, conscious, and in torment. You can't possibly twist its clear meaning.

Look closely at these next twenty-eight verses. Can anyone possibly twist all of these also?

> ▶ "The wicked shall be silent in darkness" (1 Sam. 2:9). Why mention silence if you are nonexistent?

> ▶ "He will not depart from darkness; the flame will dry out his branches" (Job 15:30). You would have to exist in order to not depart from darkness.

> ▶ "The sorrows of Sheol [hell] surrounded me" (Ps. 18:5). What sorrows would there be if you didn't exist?

> ▶ "They shall never see light" (Ps. 49:19). One must still exist to *never see* light.

> ▶ "The pangs of Sheol laid hold of me; I found trouble and sorrow" (Ps. 116:3). How could you find sorrow if you don't exist?

> ▶ "Her guests are in the depths of hell" (Prov. 9:18). How does one have guests if he or she doesn't exist?

> ▶ "They will be gathered together, as prisoners are gathered in the pit, and will be shut up in the prison" (Isa. 24:22). How could you be "shut up in the prison" if you don't exist?

▶ "Who among us shall dwell with everlasting burnings?" (Isa. 33:14). To be burnt everlastingly, you would have to exist (same word in Ps. 112:6).

▶ "It shall not be quenched night or day; its smoke shall ascend forever" (Isa. 34:10).

▶ "Those who go down to the pit cannot hope for Your truth" (Isa. 38:18). You would not need hope if you didn't exist.

▶ "For their worm does not die, and their fire is not quenched. They shall be an abhorrence to all flesh" (Isa. 66:24). How could they be "an abhorrence" if they are nonexistent?

▶ "Their everlasting confusion..." (Jer. 20:11).

▶ "He has set me in dark places like the dead of long ago" (Lam. 3:6). Unless you exist, how would you know it is dark?

▶ "For they have all been delivered to death, to the depths of the earth, among the children of men who go down to the Pit" (Ezek. 31:14). How could you be "among" if you don't exist?

▶ "...some to everlasting life, some to shame and everlasting contempt" (Dan. 12:2).

▶ "There shall be wailing and gnashing of teeth" (Matt. 13:42). One must exist to gnash teeth, and this takes place after Judgment Day.

▶ "... to be cast into the everlasting fire" (Matt. 18:8). Why everlasting fire?

▶ "Therefore you will receive greater condemnation" (Matt. 23:14). How is there a "greater" if all cease to exist?

▶ "You make him twice as much a son of hell as yourselves" (Matt. 23:15). Twice as much annihilation?

▶ "And appoint him his portion with the hypocrites" (Matt. 24:51). Why have a place assigned if you don't exist?

▶ "It is better for you to enter into life maimed, rather than having two hands, to go to hell, into the fire that shall never be quenched" (Mark 9:43). What difference would it make to have two hands in hell if you don't exist?

▶ "Their worm does not die, and the fire is not quenched" (Mark 9:44). Notice it says "their" worm. How do you have worms if you don't exist?

▶ "The chaff He will burn with unquenchable fire" (Luke 3:17). Why is unquenchable fire needed?

▶ "These shall be punished with everlasting destruction" (2 Thess. 1:9).

▶ "...for whom is reserved the blackness of darkness
   forever" (2 Pet. 2:17).

▶ "...suffering the vengeance of eternal fire" (Jude
   7). Why would fire need to be eternal if no one is in
   it?

▶ "...for whom is reserved the blackness of darkness
   forever" (Jude 13)

▶ "All liars shall have their part in the lake which
   burns with fire" (Rev. 21:8). Why would it say
   "their part" if you are nonexistent?

Jesus used the word *Gehenna* eleven times in reference to the
future hell, the hell that will exist after Judgment Day (the lake of
fire, Rev. 20:13–15). The other four times that He mentioned hell, He
used the word *Sheol*, which represents the current hell. Why would
He use the phrase "weeping and gnashing of teeth" with *Gehenna* if
people are simply *annihilated* after Judgment Day?

In Matthew 25:46, Jesus said: "And these will go away into everlasting punishment, but the righteous into eternal life." The word
for *eternal* is *aionios*. It is the same word used to describe heaven and
hell. Since those in heaven are eternal, so are those in hell. He said
the same thing in John 5:29 and Mark 16:16.

If there is no hell, then why did Jesus suffer and die for us? If hell
is only temporary, then why did Jesus warn us with forty-six verses,
especially in regard to its eternalness? How could there be varying

degrees of punishment if all cease to exist? If there is no hell, then where is the justice? These are questions that can't be answered if one believes in annihilationism or even conditional annihilation. Those verses I listed herein are so very clear. To twist so many can only be attributed to either denial or stubbornness, or rebellion.

> Annihilationism is a most serious error because it leads unrepentant sinners to underestimate their fate. Would not the ungodly be more inclined to live selfishly their whole lives, without thoughts of God, if they expected after death to face ultimate extinction rather than eternal punishment?[4]
>
> —ROBERT A. PETERSON

Understanding that hell is eternal gives us a much greater appreciation for what we were saved from. It causes us to walk more in the fear of the Lord (Prov. 16:6; Jer. 32:40; Matt. 10:28) and gives us a greater passion to witness (2 Cor. 5:10–11).

Dr. Peterson went on to say, "Studying hell…my desire that people be spared such a fate has produced in me a greater boldness to tell them the good news."[5]

Our desire should be to please God. James 4:14 says life is but a vapor. However, what we do in this minuscule moment will determine how we spend eternity. The question is: Will we be eternally minded, or will we think of only the present and not consider His desires? Our duty is to serve the Lord and warn others.

> Giving thanks to the Father who has qualified us to be partakers of the inheritance of the saints in the light. He has delivered us from the power of darkness and conveyed us into the kingdom of the Son of His love.
>
> —COLOSSIANS 1:12–13

23 *Questions*

Question 21 *How does the Christian religion differ from any other?*

For by grace you have been saved through faith, and
that not of yourselves; it is the gift of God, not of works,
lest anyone should boast.

—EPHESIANS 2:8–9

N O OTHER RELIGIOUS BOOK has undergone such intense scrutiny as the Bible, and there has never been found even one discrepancy that couldn't be cleared up with good scholarship. The Bible is the only religious book that so many have tried to destroy, outlaw, and even kill its readers. Why no other book? (See Psalms 19:7; 100:5; 117:2; 119:142; Proverbs 22:21; John 5:26; 8:40, 45; 16:13; 18:37; Romans 3:7; 9:1; Galatians 2:5; Philippians 1:18; 1 Thessalonians 2:13; 2 Timothy 3:7; 3 John 4.)

No other belief has claimed that someone died for you and has proof of that person's resurrection. Billy Graham states: "Most of the world religions are based upon philosophical thought, except for Judaism, Buddhism, Islam, and Christianity. These four are based upon personalities. Only Christianity claims resurrection for its founder."[1] That claim is certain and proven to be true.

> The fact of His resurrection…is supported by a wider variety of testimonial and other evidence than any other historical event that has ever taken place since the world began…The apostles and early Christians, by the tens of thousands, believed and preached the resurrection…Most of them suffered severely for their faith, losing their possessions and often their lives…They would hardly have persisted in their testimony unless they had been firmly persuaded, after thorough consideration of all the facts, that their Savior had conquered death! They had the

witness of the apostles, of course, and also of the "five hundred brethren at once..."

The empty tomb has never been explained, except by the bodily resurrection. If the body actually were still there, or in any other place still accessible to the Jews or Romans, they would certainly have produced it as a sure means of immediately quenching the spreading flame of the Christian faith. If the apostles or other friends of Jesus somehow had the body themselves, and thus knew He was dead, they could never have preached His resurrection as they did, knowing it would surely mean persecution for them and possibly death. No man will willingly sacrifice his life for something he knows to be a lie.[2]

There has always been a continuing vast number of people who have lost their lives for the gospel. This has been over a two-thousand-year period. There are hundreds of millions of people who attend church, worshiping Jesus every week around the world. There are countless ministries doing great works to help the poor and needy and to spread the gospel. Why would all this good continue on if it were all a lie?

All other religions tell you what *you* must do to hopefully *earn* your salvation. Christianity tells you that there is nothing you can do to earn it—it's a gift. There are no works involved.

Also, no one else has solved the issue of dealing with sin. How is that dealt with in any other religion? It is not. In *Powerful Faith-Building Quotes*, John G. Lake said: "No religion among the religions of the world has ever offered a solution for the sin problem. Jesus Christ alone has brought the solution."[3]

Also, it has been found that belief in hell is actually good for a society. There was an article on USAToday.com titled, "Fed Report: Belief in Hell Boosts Economic Growth." The article stated:

"Economists searching for reasons why some nations are richer than others have found that those with a wide belief in hell are less corrupt and more prosperous, according to a report by the Federal Reserve Bank of St. Louis."[4]

The Christian belief is also unique in that it is identified by a displaying of love. No other religion can claim such a foundation of its belief. Jesus said in John 13:34–35, "That ye love one another…By this shall all men know that ye are my disciples, if ye have love one to another" (KJV). Love is shown by so many because the Bible says in 1 John 4:8 that "God is love."

Jesus said, "My words shall not pass away" (Matt. 24:35, KJV). Many religions have added their own books or taken away from the Bible. Yet the Bible strictly forbids the adding to or the taking away from its pages (Deut. 4:2; Prov. 30:6; Rev. 22:18).

The Bible continues to be the most printed book ever in the world, even though many have sought to destroy it for two thousand years. Why is no other religious book under attack? Satan has tried, but Scriptures cannot be broken (John 10:35).

The bottom line is, we can't earn our salvation, as we are not *good enough* to gain entrance. Jesus loves us, and He gave His life for us. He didn't have to, but He chose to suffer an excruciating death in our place in order for us to be able to live with Him in His perfect kingdom. He gives us the choice—to believe that He is the Son of God or to deny Him as the Son of God. Love always gives a choice (Matt. 26:2; Mark 15:20; Luke 24:7; John 19:15; 1 Cor. 1:23; 15:3–4, 6; Eph. 2:8–9; Titus 3:5.).

> Look to Me, and be saved,
> All you ends of the earth!
> For I am God, and there is no other.
>
> —ISAIAH 45:22

23 *Questions*

Question 22 *Is it fair for someone to live a wicked life and at the last moment "get saved"?*

> *If you confess with your mouth the Lord Jesus and*
> *believe in your heart that God has raised Him from the*
> *dead, you will be saved.*
>
> —ROMANS 10:9

TO MANY, IT DOESN'T seem fair that a person could lead a wicked life right up to the last, and just prior to death become a Christian and go to heaven. We would feel that person is deserving of hell. But the truth is, we all deserve hell. Remember, salvation is not based on our good works. We all are evil in God's sight (Ps. 143:2; Rom. 3:10–12, 23). It is only repentance that brings salvation. (See also Matthew 3:2; 4:17; Luke 13:3; 15:7; 24:47; Acts 3:19; 17:30.)

The point is, for God to save an extremely wicked man on his deathbed shows how loving and forgiving our God really is. His love is far beyond ours (Rom. 5:8; Eph. 3:19). He is not trying to keep people out of heaven but to get them in. If we can get it in our minds that we can't earn our way to heaven, that it has nothing to do with our being good, then we can see how He can save a wretch at the last moment.

Look at the two malefactors (thieves) on the cross. The one said, "If You are the Christ, save Yourself and us" (Luke 23:39).

> But the other, answering, rebuked him, saying, "Do you not even fear God, seeing you are under the same condemnation? And we indeed justly, for we receive the due reward of our deeds; but this Man has done nothing wrong." Then he said to Jesus, "Lord, remember me when You come into Your kingdom." And

Jesus said to him, "Assuredly, I say to you, today you will be with Me in Paradise."

—LUKE 23:40–43

The one was humble and knew he deserved his punishment. He also knew Jesus was God. He called on Him at his last moment, and Jesus saved him. That is how loving our God is. You and I might not always be that loving, but God will. Just imagine, the other thief now has all eternity to think that he was right next to the only one who could have saved him from hell and he didn't know it—or believe it. What an eternity of the deepest regret.

I'm not saying you can plan to live any way you want and then get saved at the last. No, God knows your heart, and only true repentance with a sorrowful heart brings salvation (2 Cor. 7:9). Also, you don't know that you would even have an opportunity to get saved before you die. Many die suddenly. Do not take a chance with your soul. Once you die, it is too late. You would have an eternity to think about your foolish procrastination. Make the right choice today (Deut. 30:19).

Then he [the thief on the cross] said to Jesus, "Lord, remember me when You come into Your kingdom." And Jesus said to him, "Assuredly, I say to you, today you will be with Me in Paradise."

—LUKE 23:42–43

23 *Questions*

Question 23 *How can I be assured I won't go to hell?*

Therefore, if anyone is in Christ, he is a new creation;
old things have passed away; behold, all things have
become new.

—2 CORINTHIANS 5:17

YOU CAN BE ASSURED even this day that you will be taken to heaven and not go to this terrible place of torment. If you are at a point in life where you are ready to repent of your sins—and that means to turn away from a past sinful lifestyle—if you will confess with your mouth that Jesus is Lord and Savior of your life and believe in your heart that God has raised Him from the dead, you can be saved (Luke 13:3; Rom. 10:9–10). Jesus said in John 14:6, "I am the way, the truth, and the life: no man cometh unto the Father, but by me" (KJV). There is no other way.

If you are ready, say this prayer:

> *Dear God in heaven, I know that I have sinned, and I cannot save myself. I believe that You sent Your Son, Jesus, to die on a cross for me (John 3:16; 12:47; Rom. 5:8; 1 Cor. 15:3; Gal. 1:4). I believe He was crucified, died, and was buried, and that He rose from the dead. I ask You to forgive me of my sins. I repent. I turn away from my sins. It is because of Your shed blood (Rom. 5:9; 1 John 1:7), and not by my works (Gal. 2:16; Eph. 2:8–9; Titus 3:5), that I can be saved. Come into my heart. I receive You as my Lord and my Savior. I want to thank You, Jesus, for saving me from hell. I am now a born-again Christian, going to heaven (John 3:3; 2 Cor. 5:17). I will serve You all the days of my life. Help me to*

> *stay away from sin. Thank You for saving me, in Jesus's*
> *name, amen.*

If you said that and meant it from your heart, you are now saved and in God's family (John 1:12; 17:9–10; Gal. 3:26). You are His child. You may not realize it or feel any different, but your whole eternity has changed (Titus 1:2; Heb. 5:9; 1 John 2:25). You now begin an exciting journey, as God has a plan for your life.

It is so very important to read His Word daily, as His Word is a manual for life. It teaches us how to live and how to avoid many of life's problems. It teaches us how to obtain the blessings so that we can be a blessing to others. It teaches us that our purpose in life is to praise and worship Him and to obey Him. Tithing is one of the most important things you can do, along with having an attitude of love and forgiveness. Attending a church regularly is very important. Associate with new Christian friends, as they will help you grow in His Word. It is important that you now get water baptized, a complete submerging, as it is an outward expression of an inward experience. You have died to self and risen to a new life in Him.

There is nothing more exciting than a life of serving Him. My wife and I have been so blessed. In my forty years of serving Him, He has never let me down, not once! His desire is to bless you every day so that you can help others. He is a good God and loves you so very much. Share what you have done with others (Matt. 10:32), and go win as many souls as possible, as this is our calling (Prov. 11:30; Mark 16:15; Rom. 1:15; 10:15; 1 Thess. 2:4).

GOD BLESS YOU,
BILL AND ANNETTE WIESE

For God so loved the world that He gave His only begotten Son, that whoever believes in Him should not perish but have everlasting life.

—JOHN 3:16

Questions

Notes

Question 1: *Isn't God mean for making hell?*

1. Robert Fausset, A. R. Brown, and David Jamieson, *Jamieson, Fausset, and Brown's Commentary on the Whole Bible* (Grand Rapids, MI: Zondervan, 1973), 1342.

2. Henry M. Morris and Martin E. Clark, *The Bible Has the Answer* (Green Forest, AR: Master Books, 1976), 311.

3. Robert Peterson, *Hell on Trial* (Phillipsburg, NJ: P and R Publishing, 1995).

Question 2: *You Christians are narrow-minded; isn't there more than one way to heaven?*

1. Erwin Lutzer, *Where Was God?* (Wheaton, IL: Tyndale, 2006), 74–75.

Question 3: *Wouldn't God be mean and unloving for not allowing a good person into heaven?*

1. The Barna Group, "Beliefs: Heaven or Hell," http://www.barna.org/FlexPage.aspx?Page=Topic&TopicID=3 (accessed May 1, 2008).

Question 4: *Wouldn't you say God is unloving for sending people to hell?*

1. "The Religious and Other Beliefs of Americans 2003," The Harris Poll #11, February 26, 2003, http://www.harrisinteractive.com/harris_poll/index.asp?pid=359 (accessed December 7, 2009).

2. Nancy Missler and Chuck Missler, *Tomorrow May Be Too Late* (Coeur d'Alene, ID: Koinonia House, 2004), 61.

Question 5: *Doesn't science dictate that man came from the animal kingdom?*

1. Grant R. Jeffrey, *Creation* (Colorado Springs, CO: WaterBrook Press, 2003), 23.

2. Charles Colson and Nancy Pearcy, *How Now Shall We Live?* (Carol Stream, IL: Tyndale House Publishers, Inc., 2004), 20–21.

3. Jeffrey, *Creation*, 90.

4. Ibid., 127.

5. Ibid., 123–124.

6. Ibid., 124.

7. Ibid., 140.

8. Ibid., 127; as quoted in Roger Penrose, *The Emperor's New Mind* (New York: Oxford University Press, 2002).

9. William Lane Craig, *Reasonable Faith* (Wheaton, IL: Crossway Books, 2008), 100.

10. Henry Morris, *Defending the Faith* (Green Forest, AR: Master Books, 1999), 105.

Question 6: *Where was God when the disaster (earthquake, tsunami, hurricane, etc.) struck?*

1. Walter Ralston Martin and Jill Martin Rische, *Through the Windows of Heaven* (Nashville, TN: Broadman and Holman, 1999), 103.

2. Lutzer, *Where Was God?*

Question 8: *Seventy years of sin—does that deserve an eternity of punishment?*

1. Erwin Lutzer, *One Minute After You Die* (Chicago: Moody Publishers, 2007), 111.

2. Christopher W. Morgan and Robert A. Peterson, editors, *Hell Under Fire* (Grand Rapids, MI: Zondervan, 2004), 210.

3. Ibid.

4. Morris and Clark, *The Bible Has the Answer*, 160.

5. Lee Strobel, *The Case for Faith* (Grand Rapids, MI: Zondervan, 2000), 181.

Question 10: *Isn't preaching "hell" using scare tactics?*

1. William MacDonald, *Believer's Bible Commentary* (Nashville, TN: Thomas Nelson Publishers, Inc., 1989, 1990, 1992, 1995), 1839.

2. Robert G. Gromacki, *New Testament Survey* (Grand Rapids, MI: Baker Academic, 1974), 104.

3. Ibid., 222.

4. Jamieson, Fausset, and Brown, *Jamieson, Fausset, and Brown's Commentary on the Whole Bible*, 1240.

5. Charles Spurgeon, John Wesley, and Matthew Henry, *Parallel Commentary on the New Testament* (Chattanooga, TN: AMG Publishers, 2003), 605.

6. Morgan and Peterson, eds., *Hell Under Fire*, 216.

7. Jonathan Edwards, "Sermon XI: The Eternity of Hell Torments," in *Works of Jonathan Edwards*, vol. 2, viewed online at Christian Classics Ethereal Library, http://www.ccel.org/ccel/edwards/works2.iv.xii.html (accessed March 10, 2010).

Question 11: *Doesn't God consider my heart? I mean well!*

1. Lutzer, *Where Was God?* 54.

Question 14: *Can't God overlook my sins?*

1. Charles Stanley, *Charles Stanley's Handbook for Christian Living* (Grand Rapids, MI: Zondervan, 2008), 271–272.

Question 15: *Can't God just create another place for man to go besides hell?*

1. Edward Donnelly, *Heaven and Hell* (Carlisle, PA: Banner of Truth, 2002), 61–62.

Question 17: *Can't God just put a stop to the evil that is occurring?*

1. Morris and Clark, *The Bible Has the Answer*, 25.

Question 18: *Is the fire in hell real or metaphorical?*

1. Charles W. Draper et al., eds. *Holman Illustrated Bible Dictionary* (Nashville, TN: Holman Reference, 2003), 745–746, s.v. "Matthew 13."
2. Morris and Clark, *The Bible Has the Answer*, 74.
3. Josh McDowell and Don Stewart, *Reasons* (Wheaton, IL: Living Books, 1986), 36.

4. The use of the word *Gehenna* is verified and documented in my book *Hell* (Lake Mary, FL: Charisma House, 2008), 176–179.

Question 19: *Why are the demons themselves not in torment?*

1. Warren W. Wiersbe, *The Bible Exposition Commentary*, volume 1 (Elgin, IL: David C. Cook, 2001), 34.

2. Jamieson, Fausset, and Brown, *Jamieson, Fausset, and Brown's Commentary on the Whole Bible*, 952, s.v. "Luke 4:34."

3. Matthew Henry, *Matthew Henry's Commentary on the Whole Bible* (Peabody, MA: Hendrickson Publishers, 2005), 1652–1653.

4. Warren Wiersbe, *The Wiersbe Bible Commentary: The Complete New Testament* (Colorado Springs, CO: David C. Cook, 2007).

5. Bill Wiese, *Hell* (Lake, Mary, FL: Charisma House, 2008), 209–213.

6. Henry, *Matthew Henry's Commentary on the Whole Bible*, 1709, s.v. "Matthew 18:34."

7. Spurgeon, Wesley, and Henry, *Parallel Commentary on the New Testament*, 72, s.v. "Matthew 18:34."

8. Ibid., 76.

9. Henry, *Matthew Henry's Commentary on the Whole Bible*, 816.

10. Ibid., 1752.

11. W. E. Vine, *Vine's Expository Dictionary of Old and New Testament Words* (Nashville, TN: Thomas Nelson, 1996), 300.

12. Henry, *Matthew Henry's Commentary on the Whole Bible*, 1661.

13. Ibid., 692.

14. Jamieson, Fausset, and Brown, *Jamieson, Fausset, and Brown's Commentary on the Whole Bible*, 395.

15. Ibid., 1569.

16. Lutzer, *One Minute After You Die*, 25.

17. Henry, *Matthew Henry's Commentary on the Whole Bible*, 165.

Question 20: *Since God is a loving God, all who reject Him are anni-hilated (and not left to suffer eternally), right?*

1. Morgan and Peterson, eds., *Hell Under Fire*, 196.
2. Peterson, *Hell on Trial*, 197.
3. Wiese, *Hell*, 279.
4. Peterson, *Hell on Trial*, 178.
5. Ibid., 201.

Question 21: *How does the Christian religion differ from any other?*

1. Billy Graham, *The Classic Writings of Billy Graham* (New York: Inspirational Press, 2005), 254.

2. Morris and Clark, *The Bible Has the Answer*, 46–48.

3. Harrison House Publishers, *Powerful Faith-Building Quotes From Leading Charismatic Ministers of All Times* (Tulsa, OK: Harrison House, 1996), 151.

4. Reuters, "Fed Report: Belief in Hell Boosts Economic Growth," July 27, 2004, http://www.usatoday.com/money/economy/fed/2004-07-27 -fed-hell_x.htm (accessed January 28, 2010).

23 *Questions*

For Further Information:

Soul Choice Ministries
P. O. Box 26588
Santa Ana, CA 92799

Web site: **www.23minutesinhell.org**

FREE NEWSLETTERS
TO HELP EMPOWER YOUR LIFE

Why subscribe today?

- [ ] **DELIVERED DIRECTLY TO YOU.** All you have to do is open your inbox and read.

- [ ] **EXCLUSIVE CONTENT.** We cover the news overlooked by the mainstream press.

- [ ] **STAY CURRENT.** Find the latest court rulings, revivals, and cultural trends.

- [ ] **UPDATE OTHERS.** Easy to forward to friends and family with the click of your mouse.

CHOOSE THE E-NEWSLETTER THAT INTERESTS YOU MOST:

- Christian news
- Daily devotionals
- Spiritual empowerment
- And much, much more

SIGN UP AT: **http://freenewsletters.charismamag.com**

8178